Science Projects About
Weather

Robert Gardner
and
David Webster

• Science Projects •

Enslow Publishers, Inc.

40 Industrial Road	PO Box 38
Box 398	Aldershot
Berkeley Heights, NJ 07922	Hants GU12 6BP
USA	UK

http://www.enslow.com

Library of Congress Cataloging-in-Publication Data

Gardner, Robert, 1929-
    Science projects about weather / by Robert Gardner and David Webster.
        p. cm. — (Science projects)
    Includes bibliographical references and index.
    ISBN 0-89490-533-3
    1. Weather—Experiments—Juvenile literature. 2. Science projects—Juvenile
literature. 3. Science—Exhibitions—Juvenile literature. [1. Weather—Experiments.
2. Experiments. 3. Science projects.] I. Webster, David, 1930- . II. Title. III.
Series: Gardner, Robert, 1929- Science projects.
QC981.3.G38 1994
551.5'078—dc20   93-48720
                                            CIP
                                            AC

Printed in the United States of America

10 9 8 7 6

To Our Readers: All Internet Addresses in this book were active and appropriate
when we went to press. Any comments or suggestions can be sent by e-mail to
Comments@enslow.com or to the address on the back cover.

Illustration Credits: Stephen F. Delisle

Photo Credits: Robert Gardner, p. 34 (bottom); NOAA, pp. 84, 92; NOAA,
by Charles Watson, p. 81; David Webster, pp. 34 (top and middle), 54.

Cover Photo: © Stuart Simons, 1994

Contents

Introduction **5**

1 *The Atmosphere:*
Where Weather Is Made **9**

Pressure Changes in the Earth's Sea of Air*   12

A Spectroscope*   19

What Fraction of the Air is Oxygen?*   22

2 *Rain and Snow* **26**

A Model of the Water Cycle*   28

Evaporation*   28

Make a Cloud*   32

How Big are Raindrops?*   38

3 *Earth, Sun, Temperature, and Weather* **43**

When is the Warmest Time of Day?*   46

Absorption of Radiation Heat
by Water and by Soil*   47

Cause of the Seasons*   53

4 *Air and Wind* **56**

Can You Weigh Air?*   57

Water—Hot & Cold—Which Weighs More?*   63

Volume of Air and Temperature*   66

Motion on a Rotating Surface*   71

*appropriate for science fair project ideas

5 *Stormy Weather* **78**

    How Far Away is the Storm? 82

    Make a Liquid Tornado 86

6 *Your Weather Station* **95**

    Make a Wind Vane* 97

    Make an Anemometer* 99

    Make a Rain Gauge* 102

    Measuring Snow Depth* 104

    Measuring the Water Content of Snow* 104

    Measuring Humidity with a Hygrometer* 107

7 *Making Weather Forecasts* **112**

  Appendix: Suppliers of Materials **120**

  Bibliography **121**

  Internet Addresses **122**

  Index **127**

*appropriate for science fair project ideas

Introduction

The science projects and experiments in this book have to do with weather. Trying to understand weather and its changes is a very complicated subject. Although meteorologists (people who study weather) have learned much about the atmosphere, their short-range forecasts are often wrong. Nevertheless, only by continuing to investigate the weather and its changes can we hope to understand it.

In this book you will carry out a number of investigations designed to help you understand weather and eventually make your own forecasts. In some of the experiments you may need more than one pair of hands. When faced with such a task, ask a friend or family member to help you. He or she will probably enjoy learning more about weather.

As you do these projects, you will find it useful to record your ideas, notes, data, and anything you can conclude from your experiments in a notebook. In that way, you can keep track of the information you gather and the conclusions you reach. It will allow you to refer back to other experiments you have done that may be useful to you in projects you will do later.

Science Fairs

Some of the projects in this book might be appropriate for a science fair. Those projects are indicated with an asterisk (*). However, judges at such fairs do not reward projects or experiments that are simply copied from a book. For example, a model of a cloud would probably not impress judges unless it was done in a novel or creative way. A model that showed how raindrops form in a cloud would receive much more consideration than fluffy pieces of cotton glued to a blue background.

Science fair judges tend to reward creative thought and imagination. However, it is difficult to be creative or imaginative unless you are really interested in your project, so choose something that appeals to you. Consider, too, your own ability and the cost of materials needed for the project.

If you decide to use a project found in this book for a science fair, you will need to find ways to modify or extend the project. This should not be difficult because you will probably find that as you do these projects new ideas for experiments will come to mind. These new experiments could make excellent science fair projects, particularly because they spring from your own mind and are interesting to you.

If you decide to enter a science fair and have never done so before, you should read some of the books listed in the bibliography at the back of this book. The references that deal specifically with science fairs will provide plenty of helpful hints and lots of useful information that will enable you to avoid the pitfalls that sometimes plague first-time entrants. You will learn how to prepare appealing reports that include charts and graphs, how to set up and display your work, how to present your project, and how to relate to judges and visitors.

Safety First

Most of the projects included in this book are perfectly safe. However, the following safety rules are well worth reading before you start any project.

1. Do any experiments or projects, whether from this book or of your own design, under the supervision of a science teacher or other knowledgeable adult.

2. Read all instructions carefully before proceeding with a project. If you have questions, check with your supervisor before going any further.

3. Maintain a serious attitude while conducting experiments. Fooling around can be dangerous to you and to others.

4. Wear approved safety goggles when you are doing anything that might cause injury to your eyes.

5. Do not eat or drink while experimenting.

6. Have a first aid kit nearby while you are experimenting.

7. Do not put your fingers or any object into electrical outlets.

8. Never experiment with household electricity except under the supervision of a knowledgeable adult.

9. Do not touch a lit light bulb. Light bulbs produce light but they also produce heat.

10. Never look directly at the sun. It can cause permanent damage to your eyes.

11. If a thermometer breaks, inform your adult supervisor. Do not touch broken glass with your bare hands. Always use an alcohol thermometer, never a mercury thermometer.

12. Practice patience as you experiment. Experiments performed with care lead to results in which you can have confidence.

1

The Atmosphere: Where Weather Is Made

We live at the bottom of a vast sea of air—a sea much deeper than any ocean. The sea we live in is called the *atmosphere* to distinguish it from the seas of water—the oceans—that cover much of the earth.

Most weather takes place within 12 kilometers (7 miles) of the earth's surface. It is here that clouds form. Within these clouds, rain droplets and snow flakes may grow to sizes large enough for gravity to carry them to the bottom of the sea of air—what we call the ground. It is in the atmosphere where winds blow, temperatures change from day to day, air pressure rises and falls, and severe storms such as tornadoes, hurricanes, and thunderstorms develop.

It is on the earth's surface, at the base of the atmosphere, where our eyes sting from smog produced by automobile exhausts, industrial smoke, and temperature inversions. It is here, too, that we experience droughts, walk through fog, mud puddles, deep snow and enjoy the beauty of weather's side effects—clear blue skies, clouds that resemble fluffy cotton, fresh winds, frost–covered grass, sunsets, moon rises, rainbows, and halos.

Weather and Meteorologists

The only thing constant about the weather is that it is constantly changing. Mark Twain, who lived in various parts of the United States, spent the last years of his life in New England. He is often credited with saying, "Everybody talks about the weather, but nobody does anything about it."

Actually those words appeared in an editorial published by the *Hartford Courant* on August 24, 1897. However, Twain did have something to say about the frequent changes in weather that characterize New England's climate. In a speech to the New England Society in 1876 Twain said, "There is a sumptuous variety about New England weather that compels the stranger's admiration—and regret. The weather is always doing something there; always attending strictly to business; always getting up new designs and trying them on people to see how they will go. . . . In the spring I have counted one hundred and thirty-six different kinds of weather inside of twenty-four hours."

It is true that Mark Twain often exaggerated, but changes in weather are frequent, which is why meteorologists are hired by many private businesses, as well as by the National Weather Service, to predict the weather. Meteorologists are scientists who study the atmosphere and try to predict how it will affect the weather we experience on earth. Airlines, professional sports teams, cities concerned about pollution, fuel companies, manufacturers of consumer products and the stores that sell them, and shippers are all concerned about the weather. Of course, farmers must know about the weather in order to plan ahead; their success or failure depends largely upon the weather. Many of these firms employ meteorologists to keep them informed about aspects of the weather that are of particular concern to them. The National Weather Service hires meteorologists to provide weather information to the entire population. By listening to a public weather report you may decide to cancel a picnic or a hike, and local farmers may decide not to cut hay tomorrow.

Living in a Sea of Air

When you dive into a lake, pool, or ocean, you are aware of an increase in the pressure pushing on your body. As you ascend to the surface, you feel that the pressure exerted by the water decreases. You experience similar pressure changes in your ears when you go up and down in an elevator or in an airplane. Sometimes you have to swallow or yawn to allow the pressures to become the same on both sides of your ear drums.

If you have an aneroid barometer in your home or school, you can use it in investigation 1.1 to actually measure the air pressure as you go up and down in the earth's sea of air. From Figure 1-1a you can see how such a barometer works. Figure 1-1b is a diagram of a mercury barometer, which was invented by Evangelista Torricelli around 1643. Torricelli sealed one end of a long glass tube and then through the open end filled it with mercury. After covering the open end with his finger, he inverted the tube, and placed the open end beneath the surface of a pool of mercury in a pan. When he removed his finger, the mercury in the tube fell until it was about 76 cm (30 in) above the mercury level in the pan. Torricelli concluded that air pressure was able to support a column of mercury 76 cm (30 in) tall.

1.1 Pressure Changes in the Earth's Sea of Air*

Use an aneroid barometer to measure the air pressure on the first floor or basement of a tall building or at the base of a high hill. Then climb (or take an elevator or car) to the top floor of the building or to the hilltop and measure the air pressure again. What happens to the air pressure as you go higher into the earth's sea of air?

Things you'll need:

- aneroid barometer
- tall building or hill

Now go back to the bottom of the building or the base of the hill. What happens to the pressure as you descend deeper into the earth's sea of air?

Exploring on Your Own

- Take an aneroid barometer with you on an automobile or airplane trip. What happens to the air pressure as you go up and down in the earth's sea of air? If you are on a commercial airplane flight, why does the pressure not continue to fall as the plane climbs higher and higher?

- To see how pressure changes with depth of water, place an aneroid barometer in a *water-tight* plastic bag. To be sure the bag does not leak, fill it with air and squeeze it before you continue with the experiment. Slowly lower the barometer, within the sealed bag, into a pail or tank of water. What happens to the pressure beneath as you go deeper?

Just for Fun

- Keep a record of how the weather affects your activities and those

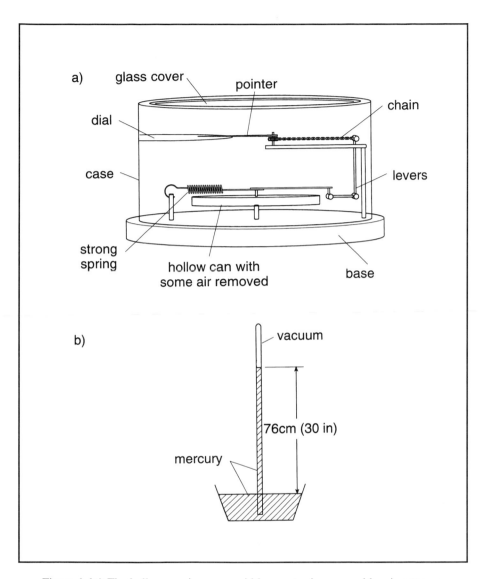

Figure 1-1a) The hollow can in an aneroid barometer is squeezed by air pressure. Changes in air pressure cause the can to expand or contract. These changes are magnified by levers that are connected to a pointer by a chain. The pointer moves over a dial from which you can read the pressure. 1-1b) When Torricelli inverted a glass tube filled with mercury in a dish of mercury, the mercury ran out of the tube until the height of the mercury in the tube was 76 cm (30 in) above the mercury level in the dish. Torricelli reasoned that air pressure was able to balance the mercury column in the tube.

of your family and school for a month. How many changes in plans were made because of the weather?

UP! UP! Into the Atmosphere

For thousands of years no one knew how far the atmosphere extended into space, but by the seventeenth century it was known that air pressure became progressively less as altitude increased. This fact was discovered by Blaise Pascal in 1648 when he asked his brother-in-law to use a mercury barometer to measure air pressure at various altitudes while climbing the Puy de Dôme Mountain in France. The barometer showed that as altitude increases, air pressure decreases. This is just what you found if you did investigation 1.1.

Other experiments showed that temperature usually decreases with altitude; however, sometimes temperature increases with altitude. When this happens, it is called a *temperature inversion.*

As people began to use balloons, then airplanes and rockets, and finally spaceships to carry people and weather instruments to ever greater heights above the earth, Pascal's discovery was confirmed again and again. Figure 1-2 shows how pressure and temperature vary with altitude. It also shows how we divide the atmosphere into layers.

In the *troposphere*, the layer of air closest to the ground, the temperature decreases as we ascend. The top of the troposphere is about 12 km (8 mi) high, but it varies with season and latitude. Near the equator, the troposphere extends about 18 km (11 mi) upward. It is only about 6 km (4 mi) high over the poles. Generally the troposphere is taller in the summer than in the winter.

As you can see from Figure 1-2, temperatures rise as we ascend through the stratosphere, decline through the mesosphere, and then rise again in the thermosphere. Pressure, on the other hand, continues to fall the higher into the atmosphere we go. For all practical purposes, the air pressure is zero in the thermosphere.

You can adjust to altitude quite easily if you fly from New York,

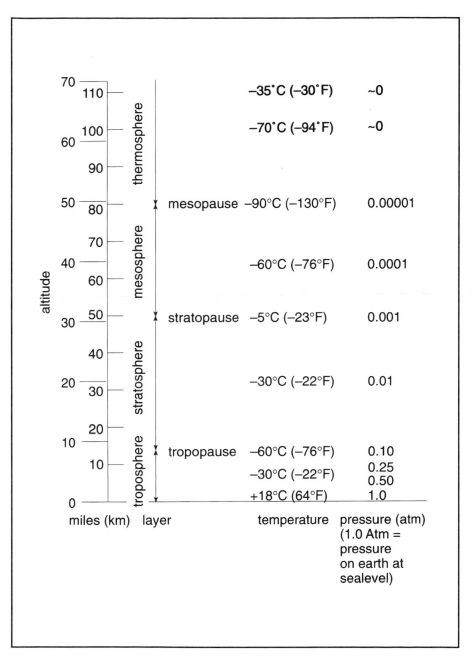

Figure 1-2) This chart shows how pressure and temperature change at different altitudes within the layers of atmosphere above the earth's surface.

Seattle, or any coastal region to Denver, the Mile-high City, where the air is 'thinner' than it is in most cities. In Denver the air pressure is only about 85 percent as great as it is at sea level. However, if you immediately drive from Denver to the 3,600 m (12,000 ft) mountains west of the city, you will find that such a simple task as walking increases your breathing and heart rates dramatically. The pressure on these Rocky Mountains is only about two-thirds as great as at sea level. This means that you breathe only two-thirds as much oxygen with each breath. Is it any wonder that you have to breathe faster to get the oxygen you need?

With time, you can adjust to changes in altitude. You become *acclimated* to the reduced pressure. Your body slowly develops more red blood cells, which enables you to carry more oxygen from your lungs to the cells of your body. You also breathe more deeply and, therefore, more oxygen enters your lungs. The people who live in the Andes Mountains of South America are able to work at an altitude of 5,800 m (19,000 ft) without ill effects. At this altitude, the air pressure and the concentration of oxygen are both less than half that which exist at sea level. Blood tests show that these people have red blood cell counts of 8 million per cubic millimeter of blood. (A count of 4.8 million per cubic millimeter is normal.) In addition, these people develop larger lungs with more surface area through which oxygen can move from inhaled air into their blood.

Mountain climbers can acclimate to mountains as high as Mount McKinley's 6,200 m (20,320 ft) peak, but auxiliary oxygen is essential for climbers seeking the 8,850 m (29,028 ft) summit of Mount Everest—an altitude where jet airplanes sometimes cruise.

Within commercial airplanes, which fly at altitudes of 10 km (6 mi) or more, the air pressure must be higher than the pressure outside the plane to prevent passengers from developing high altitude sickness. Aboard Skylab in 1973, the air pressure in the space station was only one-third normal atmospheric pressure. This corresponds to an altitude on earth of 8.3 km (5.2 mi). Normally, people cannot live at such an altitude; yet, astronauts worked effectively on board Skylab. The air they breathed was 70 percent oxygen instead of 21 percent as it is in ordinary air.

Atmospheres in the Solar System

A visitor from another galaxy would probably be surprised to find that of all the planets circling our Sun, only Earth has an atmosphere rich in oxygen. Space probes launched from Earth have taken samples of the atmospheres of Venus and Mars, analyzed the data, and transmitted the information back to Earth. But even before these probes were launched, we knew what gases made up their atmospheres. The sunlight reflected from the planets and stars can be examined with a spectroscope. Usually a photograph is taken of the colored lines produced by the light passing through the spectroscope. Because different gases produce and absorb different colors, the gases present in a planet's atmosphere can be determined. In a similar way, the gases present in very distant stars can be determined as well.

Mercury, the planet closest to the Sun, has virtually no atmosphere because of its weak gravity. Most of the gases that were on this planet have escaped and spread through space. Venus, which circles the Sun between the orbits of Earth and Mercury, is covered by a thick layer of clouds containing droplets of sulfuric acid. Its atmosphere is 95 percent carbon dioxide, with some nitrogen, and traces of oxygen, argon, and water vapor.

We cannot see the surface of Venus because the clouds in its atmosphere reflect most of the sunlight that strikes them. However, space probes sent to Venus reveal a planet very different from ours. The pressure of the atmosphere at the surface of Venus is 90 times greater than the pressure of the air we live in, and the temperature there is about 480°C (900°F)—nearly as hot as a burning match! Venus is hot because of its carbon dioxide-rich atmosphere which creates a *greenhouse effect*.

Mars, the next planet beyond Earth, has an atmosphere that is, again, practically all carbon dioxide. Unlike Venus, the pressure of the Martian atmosphere is only one-hundredth as great as ours, and the temperature there varies from 20°C (70°F) to a frigid -140°C (-220°F). Most of the water on Mars, which may have flowed over its surface at some point in its history, is now frozen, and its white polar caps are probably a mixture of ice (frozen water) and dry ice (frozen carbon dioxide). What were once thought to be clouds circling the surface of the 'Red Planet' turned out to be giant dust storms that grow over a period of six weeks and then take 3 or 4 times as long to subside. Such dust storms make it clear that winds are not unknown on Mars. For so thin an atmosphere to generate such storms, the particles of red dust moved by the winds must be extremely small.

The outer or Jovian planets—Jupiter, Uranus, and Neptune—are much larger and far less dense than the inner Terrestrial planets (Mercury, Venus, Earth, and Mars). Their atmospheres consist primarily of hydrogen mixed with some helium. Pluto, the outermost planet, is very small and, like Mercury, lacks the gravity needed to hold an atmosphere.

During experiment 1.2, you will have an opportunity to build a spectroscope of your own. Because the light from planets and stars is very dim, you probably will not be able to analyze the light that comes from them. However, you will be able to see how a simple spectroscope works by using brighter sources of light. (Astronomers use photographic film at the ends of their spectroscopes to make long-exposure time photographs of the light from stars and planets.)

1.2 A Spectroscope*

Many spectroscopes contain a diffraction grating. A diffraction grating is an inexpensive device that will separate light into colors. It consists of many narrow slits arranged side by side. When light passes through these slits, it gets spread out into the colors that make up the light. Your school may have

Things you'll need:

- diffraction grating
- black construction paper
- cardboard tube such as a mailing tube or toilet paper roll
- scissors

diffraction gratings. If not, you can buy them from a science supply house or a hobby shop.

Look at the light from a light bulb through a diffraction grating. Hold the grating close to your eye. Turn the grating until you see colored light spread out horizontally at each side of the grating.

You can build a spectroscope as shown in Figure 1-3. Then look at a light bulb through the spectroscope you have made. What colors do you see? Now look at the light from a fluorescent light tube through your spectroscope. Turn the spectroscope so that its slit is parallel with the fluorescent tube. You will see all the colors in the rainbow. Superimposed on these colors you can also see the bright colored lines produced by the mercury vapor inside the tube. What are the colors of these lines?

Use your spectroscope to examine the light from colored light bulbs, red neon signs, other colored light signs, and the light from mercury and sodium vapor lamps. Your spectroscope will not separate the dim light from stars or planets, but you can look at moonlight or a distant street lamp or porch light. **DO NOT look at sunlight with your spectroscope! Sunlight is so bright that it can damage your eyes.**

Earth's Atmosphere

Earth's atmosphere, most of which lies in the troposphere, is very

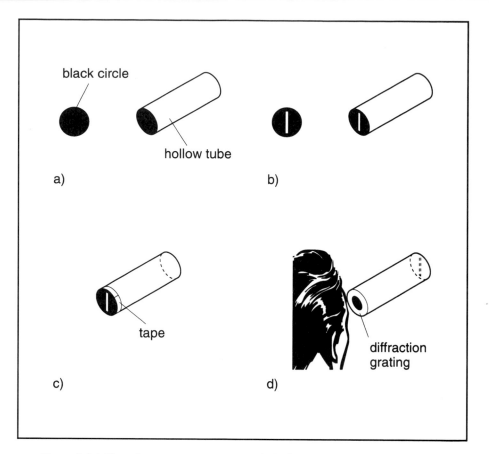

a)

black circle

hollow tube

b)

c)

tape

d)

diffraction grating

Figure 1-3a) To make a spectroscope, cut a circle from a roll of black construction paper. The circle should be a little larger in diameter than the mailing tube (or the empty tube from a roll of toilet paper). 1-3b) Use scissors to cut a narrow slit along the circle's diameter. 1-3c) Tape the black circle to one end of the tube. 1-3d) Cover the other end with a diffraction grating. Look at a light bulb though the grating and the slit. Keep the slit vertical. Turn the grating until the light turns into colored bands on each side of the slit. Fix the grating in position by taping it in place.

different from those of the other planets in our solar system. It consists of about 78 percent nitrogen, 21 percent oxygen, and a little less than one percent argon. While two-thirds of the earth's surface is covered with liquid water, water vapor makes up only a small fraction of the atmosphere. And, unlike the atmospheres of Venus and Mars, carbon dioxide is only 0.035 percent of our atmosphere. However, even so small a fraction of carbon dioxide traps a large amount of heat that would otherwise escape into space.

Another gas found in small quantities high in our atmosphere is ozone—a form of oxygen. (Unlike ordinary oxygen molecules, which consist of two atoms, ozone molecules are made up of three oxygen atoms.) Most of the ozone is found in the stratosphere about 12-50 km (7-30 mi) above the earth's surface. Although there is relatively little of this gas in the atmosphere, it serves a very important function. It absorbs much of the ultraviolet light that is present in sunlight. (It is the absorption of ultraviolet rays from the sun that warms this region of the atmosphere.) Ultraviolet light is capable of damaging living cells, which is why it is sometimes used to destroy harmful bacteria. However, it can also damage cells in our skin and causes some forms of skin cancer. There is evidence that some ozone is being destroyed by gases such as freon, which is used in spray cans, air conditioners, and for a variety of other purposes.

The high concentration of oxygen—one of the many gases that animals breathe—makes life on Earth possible. The Viking landers that probed the Martian surface found no evidence of life. It is likely that Earth's oxygen-rich atmosphere and the abundance of water on its surface provides the only environment in the solar system that can support life. It is this same combination of air and water, together with the Sun's energy and Earth's rotation, that makes our weather.

To find out how much of the air is oxygen, you can remove oxygen from a sample of air and see how much is left. You can do this because oxygen, unlike nitrogen, is a very reactive element. It combines with many substances. For example, charcoal, which is mostly carbon, burns when it reacts with oxygen to form carbon dioxide gas. Many other substances, such as wood, leaves, and sulfur also burn when they combine with the oxygen in air. On the other hand, iron reacts slowly with oxygen to form iron oxide, a compound known to you as rust.

You can use the rusting of iron to find out what fraction of the air is oxygen. You will do this in project 1.3.

1.3 What Fraction of the Air is Oxygen?*

Because steel wool is mostly iron, it reacts with oxygen just as iron does. Roll some strands of steel wool into a small ball. Make several such balls of steel wool. These balls should be slightly wider than the diameter of the narrow jar or test tube you plan to use. To remove the thin coating of oil that covers most steel wool, soak it for about a minute in vinegar. Then shake the vinegar off the steel wool.

Things you'll need:

- steel wool
- vinegar
- water with a drop or two of food coloring
- tall narrow jar (such as an olive jar) or large test tube
- shallow dish
- container to hold vinegar
- ruler

Use a pencil to push one small ball of steel wool to the bottom of a tall narrow jar or a test tube. Turn the tube or jar upside down and place it in a shallow dish of colored water. Be sure the mouth of the jar is covered with water as shown in Figure 1-4.

Every few hours examine the inverted jar and steel wool. Then leave it in place overnight. Why does the water level in the jar rise as the steel wool reacts with the oxygen in the air? When the water stops rising in the jar, use a ruler to measure the total height of the jar and the height of the water in the jar. What fraction of the air originally in the jar reacted with the steel wool? Look at the steel wool. What evidence do you have that the steel wool has reacted chemically with the oxygen that was in the tube?

Repeat the experiment several times. Are the results consistent? How does your value for the fraction of the air that is oxygen compare with the 21 percent value given above?

Exploring on Your Own

- When a candle burns, it combines with the oxygen in the air. If you

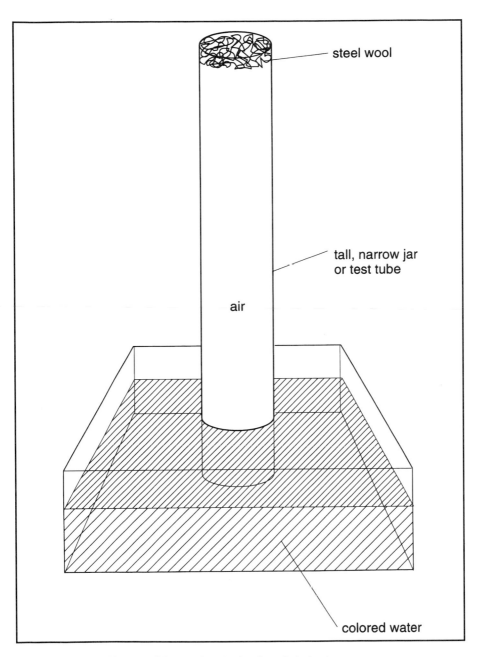

Figure 1-4) Measuring the fraction of air that is oxygen.

place a jar over a burning candle, you know that the candle will go out after a short time. But how long will it burn? To find out, support a candle with a small piece of clay or some melted wax as shown in Figure 1-5a. Then **ask an adult to help you light the candle and cover it with a jar** (Figure 1-5b). How long does the candle continue to burn? If you use a bigger jar, do you predict that the candle will burn for a longer time, for less time, or for the same time? What happens if you use a smaller jar? **Ask an adult to help you test your predictions.**

- **Now with adult help** repeat the experiment you did in investigation 1.3 once more. Push a small ball of steel wool that has been rinsed with vinegar to the bottom of the tall, narrow jar or test tube before it is inverted over a burning candle. When the candle goes out and

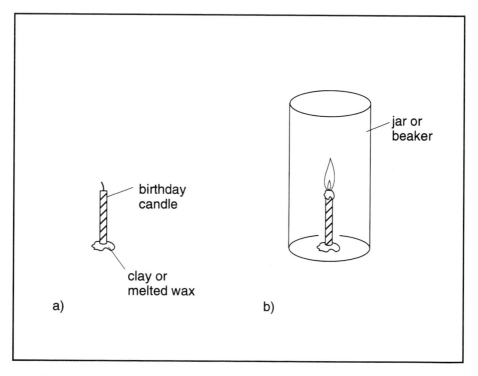

Figure 1-5) How does the amount of air around a candle affect the time it will burn?

water stops rising in the jar, mark the water level on the jar with a marking pen or a piece of tape. (See Figure 1-6.) Watch the water level over the next 24 hours. How can you explain the rise in the water level? Look closely at the steel wool. Is there evidence that it has reacted? Did the candle use up all of the oxygen in the jar when it burned?

You now know what we meant at the beginning of this chapter when we said that we live at the bottom of a vast sea of air. Now that the stage has been set, we will begin to explore different aspects of weather. In Chapter 2 you will have a chance to investigate the way water moves to and from the air, making weather as it goes.

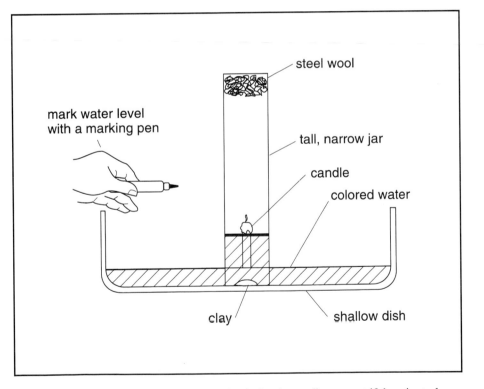

Figure 1-6) What happens to the water level after the candle goes out if there is steel wool in the jar?

2

Rain and Snow

If you are like most people, you probably do not like rain. But without it the earth would not be a very nice place to live. There would be no rivers or lakes. All the land would be covered with dry deserts. Plants and animals could exist only in the oceans or on the nearby shores.

In the beginning, the earth was just a giant blob of molten rock surrounded by a dense cloud of steam. The earth cooled slowly as its heat dissipated into space. Then it started to rain. What a rainstorm! It lasted for millions of years. As soon as the rain touched the hot ground, the water boiled away into the air as steam.

At last, the earth cooled enough to allow the rain to form rivers, lakes, and oceans. Our planet was ready for the evolution of plant and animal life.

The Water Cycle

Today, rain water still returns from the earth to the atmosphere. The sun's heat causes water to evaporate as invisible water vapor. As moist air cools, the water vapor condenses to form a cloud of tiny water droplets. As the droplets grow in size, they become heavy enough to fall as rain or snow.

This continual process of evaporation, condensation, and precipitation (rain or snow) is known as the water cycle. Cycle means circle. The earth's water moves in a giant cycle from the clouds, to the earth as rain or snow, and then back again into the atmosphere. (See Figure 2-1.) The water in the rain that falls on you once fell on the backs of dinosaurs!

In the next investigation you will make a model of the water cycle in your kitchen or classroom.

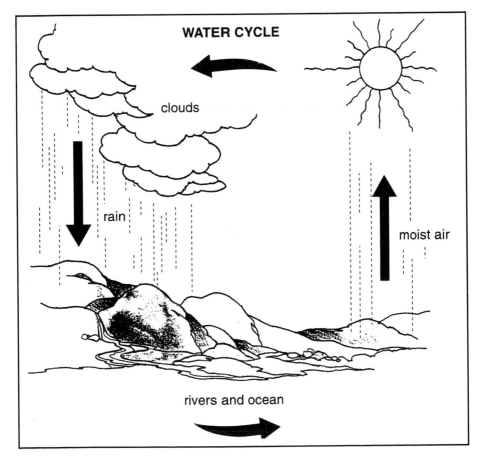

Figure 2-1) Water evaporates into the air and returns as rain or snow.

2.1 A Model of the Water Cycle*

Ask an adult to help you with this experiment. Remove the label from a tin can and fill it with ice water. Put about an inch of water in a sauce pan. Heat the pan on a stove or hot plate until the water begins to boil. Then hold the can of ice water about 15 cm (6 in) above the pan. You will see steam condensing as a mist on the outside of the cold can. Soon a few drops will become large enough to fall back into the pan. It is raining above your stove.

Things you'll need:

- tin can
- ice
- water
- sauce pan
- stove or hot plate

Evaporation

If boiling water is left on a hot stove, all the water will soon evaporate into the air. You know that an unfolded paper towel dries much faster than a wadded up one. Wind, also, causes evaporation to occur more rapidly.

In the next investigation you will measure how fast water evaporates from two different containers.

2.2 Evaporation*

Use a measuring cup or a graduated cylinder to pour 60 mL (2 oz) of water into a drinking glass. Then pour the same amount of water into a wide soup bowl. Put the containers next to each other in a place where you will notice them each day.

Things you'll need:

- small drinking glass
- wide soup bowl
- measuring cup or graduated cylinder

How long do you think it will take for the water to evaporate from each container? Do you think it will take longer for the water to evaporate from the glass or from the bowl? Record your predictions in your notebook. Ask some family members or friends to make predictions too. Maybe you could even offer a prize to the person who makes the best estimate.

Is evaporation without heat a slow process? Why does the water evaporate faster from one container than from the other?

Exploring on Your Own

- Pour about 10 grams (10 mL) of water into a saucer. Into an identical saucer pour 10 grams (12 mL) of rubbing alcohol. Which liquid do you think will evaporate faster?

- Place a wet, wadded up, paper towel on one side of a balance and weigh the towel. Continue to weigh the towel every 5 minutes for an hour. How fast, in grams per minute, does water evaporate from the towel? Does the evaporation rate change with time? Now repeat the experiment, but this time spread out the towel rather than wadding it up. How does the rate of evaporation of water from the spread-out-towel compare with the rate from the wadded-up-towel?

- Design an experiment to see how wind affects the evaporation rate of water.

Just for Fun

- Spread some warm water on the back of your hand. Then wave your hand back and forth through the air. Notice that where the water is, your hand feels cool. Spread a little rubbing alcohol on your hand and do the same thing.

Condensation

Condensation occurs when moist air is cooled because cold air can hold less water vapor than warm air. For the same reason, dew forms on grass and cars during the night as the air cools near the ground. Shortly after sunrise, when the air gets warmer, the dew evaporates.

Dew is not likely to form if it is windy. Moving air stays warmer since it does not remain in contact with the cool ground very long. Also, dew rarely occurs on cloudy nights because there is less cooling due to radiation from the ground. The clouds reflect much of the radiation back to the ground.

Have you ever seen dew inside your house? You have, when you drink a glass of cold milk or soda. The outside of the glass becomes covered with tiny beads of water. Water vapor in the air condenses as it comes into contact with the cold glass.

If you live where it is cold, you see condensation outside during the winter. When you breathe out, the moisture in your breath condenses into a fine mist and you can 'see your breath.'

When the temperature is below freezing, water vapor condenses as frost instead of dew. What a beautiful sight to see the tiny ice crystals of frost sparkling in the early morning sunlight!

Just for Fun

- Have you ever noticed car tracks or footprints left in the grass when it was covered with frost? Look at the tracks again in a few days. Has the grass died and turned black?

- Another way to see condensation is to make a small terrarium in a large–mouth jar. Dig up a few small weeds and plant them in the jar. Add a little water and screw on the lid. Place the terrarium in a sunny window. Watch the terrarium to see how long the plants will live in the sealed jar without adding any water. Notice that sometimes small water drops form on the inside of the terrarium jar. The air in the jar becomes saturated with water that evaporates from the soil and plant leaves. Later, the invisible water vapor in the air condenses on the cooler glass.

Cloud formation

A cloud is just a huge mass of condensed water vapor. The vapor is carried upward by warm air that rises into the atmosphere. As warm air rises, it expands and cools. The cold air cannot hold as much water vapor. Some of the water vapor begins to condense around very small particles to form water droplets.

Most of the particles on which the vapor condenses come from the ocean. Breaking waves create bubbles that burst and eject tiny particles of sea salts into the atmosphere.

The tiny water droplets that form around the salt particles are too light to fall in the strong air currents. But they mature into larger raindrops as the smaller droplets bump together and gradually grow large enough to fall to the ground as rain. A raindrop contains about 1,000,000 cloud droplets.

When the upper air temperature is very cold, the water vapor freezes into small ice crystals, which grow bigger by colliding with smaller water droplets near them. Dropping through the bottom of the cloud, the ice crystals can melt into rain or fall as snowflakes. Whether it is rain or snow depends on the temperature of the air.

Jet airplanes make clouds known as contrails. The exhaust from jet engines contains a lot of water vapor that condenses in the cold upper air. If the air is very dry, the contrails evaporate quickly and disappear.

You can make a cloud for yourself by carrying out investigation 2.3.

2.3 Make a Cloud*

You may have seen a miniature cloud when you have opened a can or bottle of cold soda on a hot day. The cloud might appear briefly just above the opening. When you opened the can, the gas pressure inside was released. The sudden drop in pressure caused cooling that led the vapor to condense.

Here is how to make a cloud in a bottle (Figure 2-2):

(1) Put about one cup of water into the jug.

Things you'll need:

- air pump—the kind used to blow up a bike tire or inflate an air mattress
- one-gallon glass jug
- one-hole rubber stopper fitted with a short piece of glass tubing
- short piece of rubber tubing
- matches
- flashlight

(2) **With an adult to help you,** drop a few lighted matches into the jug to make smoke. The water will condense on the tiny smoke particles.

(3) Put on the stopper and shake up the jug to make the air inside moist.

(4) Attach the pump to the glass tube using the rubber tubing.

(5) Pump 2 or 3 times to increase the pressure inside the jug.

(6) Shine the flashlight into the jug.

(7) While looking into the jug, pull out the stopper quickly. You should see a cloud, but it will last for only a few seconds.

When the stopper is pulled from the jug, the pressure is lowered suddenly. The expanding air cools enough to cause the water vapor in the air to condense on the smoke particles, which take on the role of particles of sea salts in real clouds.

Kinds of Clouds

There are many different kinds of clouds. Meteorologists classify clouds into three main types: cirrus, cumulus, and stratus.

Cirrus clouds are the highest, forming 8 km (5 mi) or more above the earth. Since air temperatures at such a height are always below freezing, cirrus clouds are composed entirely of ice crystals.

Cirrus clouds, like the ones in the photograph, are easy to recognize because of their thin, wispy appearance. When blown into feathery strands, cirrus clouds are nicknamed 'mares' tails.' Sunlight passing through cirrus ice crystals can form the 'ring' or halo that is sometimes seen around the sun or moon.

Cumulus clouds are the puffy, fair weather clouds common on warm summer afternoons. The tops of cumulus clouds reflect the brilliant white sunlight, while their bases are darker because they are shaded by the clouds above. Some of these clouds are big; it might be 3.2 or 4.8 km (2 or 3 mi) from the top to the bottom of a cumulus cloud.

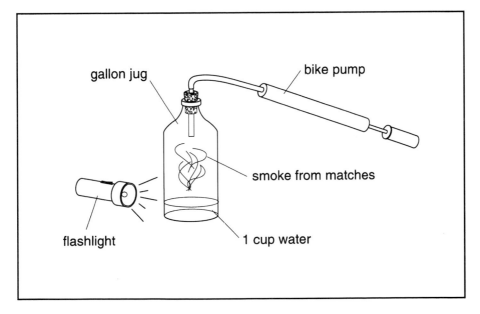

Figure 2-2) How to create a model cloud inside a bottle.

Cirrus clouds (top); Cumulus clouds (middle); Stratus clouds (bottom).

There are long names for different kinds of cumulus clouds. *Alto* is the Latin word for high, so altocumulus clouds are higher. Strato-cumulus are gray masses of layered clouds that often signal the approach of bad weather.

Stratus clouds usually blanket the entire sky and bring rain or snow. They are low clouds that stay within 1.6 km (1 mi) of the earth's surface.

Cloud Watching

It is not easy to identify many of the clouds you will see. Your library may have a book on weather with good cloud photographs. Wispy cirrus clouds and fluffy cumulus clouds may be the easiest to recognize. Can you ever see more than one kind of cloud at the same time?

Clouds can help you predict the weather. A weather change often is indicated by a change in clouds.

Cumulus clouds are the fair weather clouds seen on warm summer afternoons. But if conditions are right, a cumulus cloud can grow into a towering thunderhead called a cumulonimbus. Violent updrafts of wind may lift the top of a storm cloud as high as 19 km (12 mi) above the earth.

Cirrus clouds often signal the approach of rain. Because cirrus clouds are so high, they do not appear to move very fast.

Dark stratus clouds are usually within 1.6 km (1 mi) of the earth's surface. They form when the air is laden with water droplets, and usually accompany rain.

Exploring on Your Own

- Have you ever watched the clouds? Find a spot in an open field or on the top of a hill where you can see a lot of the sky. Lie down and watch the clouds. It is fun to look for clouds that have special shapes. Perhaps you can imagine a witch's face, a fish, or a sailing ship.

- Which way are the clouds moving? Low clouds appear to float along faster than high clouds. Do clouds always move in the same direction that the wind is blowing on the ground?

- Watch the same cloud for a long time. Does it change shape more on the top or on the bottom? See if you can spot a cloud that slowly gets bigger or one that gets smaller.

Cloud Seeding

For a long time people wondered why clouds sometimes brought rain and other times did not. During droughts, many Native American tribes would have rain dances. They thought that if they danced long enough, the gods would bring rain.

Later, pioneer rainmakers tried to coax water from the clouds by banging on big drums and making smoky fires. Some even exploded aerial bombs in a useless attempt to jar raindrops from the clouds.

Today, meteorologists know that a cloud will not produce rain unless it contains particles of salt or dust on which moisture can collect. When clouds are 'seeded,' artificial particles are spread into the clouds from an airplane. The chemicals used are either crystals of silver iodide, or finely ground dry ice, which has a temperature of -78°C (-108°F).

Cloud seeding only works when the cloud conditions are almost right for natural precipitation. It is not possible to produce rain from fair-weather cumulus clouds. Seeding can sometimes cause more rain to fall from rain clouds than would have fallen if the clouds had been left undisturbed. Unfortunately, most of the time seeding does not work at all.

Raindrops

Most people think raindrops are tear-shaped. But they are not. A raindrop is really shaped much like a hamburger bun with a flattened bottom and rounded top. Raindrops fall much too fast for you to see their shape.

Exploring on Your Own

- It is easy to see water drops on wax paper or aluminum foil. Wet your hand, and sprinkle some water on a piece of wax paper. Look at the drops from the side. You should notice that the small drops are almost perfectly spherical, but the larger ones are flattened.

- You can make a big drop by combining smaller drops. Move a lot of drops together using a pencil point. What happens to a drop's shape as it becomes larger? The rounded shape of drops is caused by surface tension. The surface of a liquid acts as if it were covered with an invisible elastic 'skin.' The skin squeezes small water drops into the smallest possible space—a sphere. Larger drops are flattened out as the force of gravity overcomes some of the surface tension.

- You can see surface tension form drops with a bucket of water. Go outside and throw a bucket of water up into the air. As the water falls, it begins to break apart as surface tension pulls the water together, pinching off drops of all sizes.

- You can also make drops inside with a sink faucet. Turn on the water and slowly turn it off until there is just a thin stream. Can you see the water pull together to form drops?

During investigation 2.4 you will find a way to capture, preserve, and compare the sizes of raindrops.

2.4 How Big are Raindrops?*

Here is how you can capture and preserve some raindrops:

Things you'll need:

- flour
- shallow pan

(1) Put about 0.6 cm (0.25 in) of flour into a pan.

(2) Cover the pan and carry it outside when it is raining (**not in a thunderstorm).**

(3) Remove the cover for just a few seconds. Each raindrop will form a small pellet of dough.

(4) Let the pellets dry for an hour, or **ask an adult to help you bake them in an oven at a very low temperature.**

(5) Separate the pellets by shaking the flour through a strainer.

Are all the pellets the same size? Do the raindrops from different storms have different sizes?

Rainbows

Have you ever seen a rainbow? Rainbows usually occur just as the sun comes out after a shower. From an airplane, it is possible to see a rainbow in a complete circle.

Sunlight is a combination of the rainbow colors: red, orange, yellow, green, blue, and violet. When light passes through raindrops, it is reflected and bent, or refracted. Since different colors are bent different amounts, the colors are separated and form a spectrum, or rainbow.

Exploring on Your Own

- You can create your own rainbow with a garden hose. Adjust the hose nozzle to make a fine spray. Then stand with your back to the sun, and squirt the spray in front of you. Move the hose around slowly until you see a rainbow.

- You can make a spectrum inside with a mirror and a clear, rectangular dish of water. Fill the dish with water and place it near a sunny window. Place the mirror against one side of the dish so part of it is under the water as shown in Figure 2-3. Look along the wall or ceiling for a colorful reflection. If necessary, turn the dish and adjust the mirror until you see the spectrum. Can you see all the rainbow colors in the spectrum? Find a bright spot on the wall or ceiling that is not colored. Where does this bright spot come from?

Just for Fun

- If you can get a prism, use it to make a spectrum by holding it in sunlight.

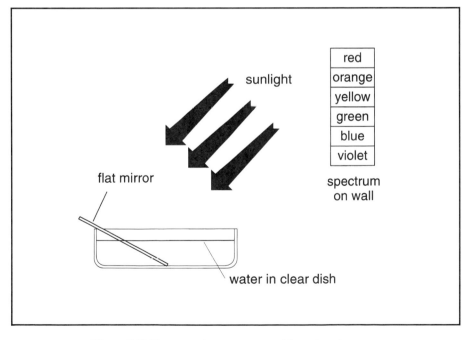

Figure 2-3) How to make a spectrum with a mirror in water.

- Look for the spectrum that forms when sunlight shines into a fish tank.

Acid rain

Acid rain has become a serious pollution problem. It is caused by factories and power plants that burn certain kinds of coal for fuel. Sulfur fumes in the burning coal combine with oxygen in the air to form sulfur dioxide gas, which in turn combines with water in the air to make sulfuric acid.

When the acid from polluted rain becomes concentrated in lakes, fish and other aquatic life can no longer survive. Acid rain also corrodes buildings made of marble rock; many ancient structures in Italy and Greece are crumbling.

Of course, not all acids are harmful. Some of the things you eat, such as orange juice and vinegar in salad dressing, are acidic. And your stomach juices contain powerful hydrochloric acid which aids in the digestion of food.

Exploring on Your Own

- Litmus or pH paper is used to test for acids and bases. Neutral litmus turns red with acid and blue with base. If you can get some litmus or pH paper, use it to test the acidity in rainwater and water from ponds and streams.

Hail

Have you ever been in a hailstorm? How strange to have ice fall from the sky on a hot summer day! It shows how cold the air is high above the earth.

The heavy storm clouds that produce hail may tower 13 km (8 mi) above the ground. At this height, the temperature of the thin air is always well below freezing. Strong winds inside the clouds blow the water droplets up and down as they freeze. The ice pellets increase in size until they fall to the ground as hail.

Hailstones are usually small (about the size of peas), but sometimes they are as large as moth balls, golf balls, or even baseballs. A hailstone once fell in Nebraska that was 41.6 cm (17 in) around and weighed 0.68 kg (1.5 lbs). How would you like that ice ball to hit you on the head?

Hailstorms can cause a lot of damage. Farm crops are flattened and apples knocked to the ground. Larger hailstones dent automobiles and break windshields. In 1932, two hundred people in China were killed by giant hailstones.

Just for Fun

- If you are ever in a hailstorm, you might want to collect some hailstones. Put them quickly in a plastic container so they do not melt in your hands. Store the hail in your freezer so you can show your friends the size of the pellets.

- Cut open one of your hailstones to find out what it looks like inside. Sometimes the layers of ice in a hailstone resemble the inside of an onion.

Snow

It often snows in the summer . . . but no one sees it. The snow forms in the cold clouds, but melts as it falls through the warmer air near the earth. In winter, however, snow, can remain frozen all the way to the ground.

A snowflake is one of nature's most beautiful gifts. The first person known to study snowflakes was Wilson Bentley, a farmer who lived in Vermont 100 years ago. He took thousands of photographs of snow crystals, and his photographs are still used today.

Exploring on Your Own

You can study snowflakes yourself with a magnifying glass. The next time it snows, go outside and catch some flakes on the sleeve of your jacket. Then look at them with a magnifier. You will have to hold your breath while looking, or the delicate crystals might melt.

If you are lucky, you will find some nicely-formed crystals that will look like the snowflake pictures. But the snow in many storms is just an assortment of uninteresting rods and pellets.

When first formed, all snowflakes have some kind of six-sided, or hexagon, arrangement. On the way down, they bump into other flakes and might break or get stuck together. When passing through layers of warmer air the thinner parts of the crystal can melt. Most snowflakes that reach the ground are not perfectly shaped.

A snowflake.

3

Earth, Sun, Temperature, and Weather

Though it looks like a small, hot ball as it drifts across the sky, the Sun is actually a star with a diameter of nearly 1,400,000 km (880,000 mi). This is more than 100 times the diameter of the earth. Like most stars, the Sun is continually emitting vast amounts of energy. Only a small amount of that energy reaches Earth, but without it there would be no life or weather as we know it on our planet.

Heat from the Sun

The Sun is the source of almost all of Earth's heat, even though it is about 150,000,000 km (93,000,000 mi) away. The temperature of the Sun's surface is about 5,800°C (11,000°F), while at its center it is about 16,000,000°C (26,000,000°F). The Sun's heat is produced by a continual atomic reaction as hydrogen atoms are joined (fused) to produce helium atoms. The Sun is changing matter into energy so fast that its weight decreases by some 4,000,000 tons every second. Nevertheless, the Sun is so big that astronomers expect it will continue to provide heat and light for another 6 billion years.

The temperatures on other planets are much different than those on Earth. Mercury is the hottest planet since it is the closest to the Sun. Temperatures on the side of Mercury facing the Sun range from 300°C (500°F) to 430°C (780°F). The average temperature on Mars is about 0°C (32°F). Its surface is comfortably warm at noon (20°C or 68°F), but becomes intensely cold (-140°C or -220°F) at night.

Daytime temperatures on the Moon reach 100°C (212°F). But at night, the temperature drops to -150°C (-240°F) as its heat is lost into space. Sunbathing would be impossible on the Moon. If you lay in the sunlight, your blood would boil. And if you hid for protection in the shadow of a rock, you would freeze almost instantly.

How much does the temperature change where you live? During the summer it might be 30°C (90°F) during the day and cool off to 20°C (70°F) at night. Even temperature changes from summer to winter are not really extreme. If you live in the South, your winter temperatures might average only 30°C (50°F) colder than the summer temperatures. The warmest temperature ever recorded in the U.S. is 57°C (134°F) in Death Valley, California. The record cold temperature is -60°C (-76°F) up in Alaska.

One reason for Earth's moderate temperature is its distance from the Sun. Earth would be a lot hotter if it were as close to the Sun as Mercury. Of course, planets that are farther from the Sun are much colder.

But the Moon is about the same distance from the Sun as Earth. Why, then, does it have such extreme temperatures?

The same side of the Moon faces the Sun for a long time, making this side very hot and the shaded side extremely cold. Luckily for us, Earth rotates every 24 hours. Your house warms up during the day, but cools off every night.

The Moon has no air since its gravity is too weak to hold it. On Earth, the thick layer of air acts as a blanket at night and prevents some heat from escaping into space.

Winds on Earth circulate air masses of different temperatures.

Warm air often moves into colder regions and makes them warmer, while cold air blows into warmer regions and cools them.

Another reason for the Moon's temperature extremes is its lack of water. The oceans and other large bodies of water absorb and retain heat and thereby modify local temperatures. This prevents the wide extremes in temperature that occur on the Moon.

The graph in Figure 3-1 shows the temperatures recorded in Boston each hour on October 6, 1990. When was it warmest? How cold did it get during the night? During investigation 3.1 you will make a similar graph of the temperature throughout the day near your home or school and find the warmest time of the day.

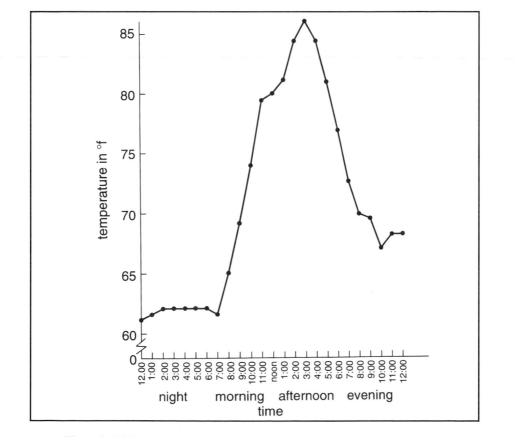

Figure 3-1) Hourly temperatures in Boston, Massachusetts on October 6, 1990.

3.1 When is the Warmest Time of Day?*

All you will need to measure temperatures where you live is a thermometer. Perhaps you have a thermometer attached to the outside of your house. If not, you could buy an inexpensive thermometer at a hardware store.

Things you'll need:

- thermometer

- graph paper

- clock or watch

Your temperature measurements should be made on a nice sunny day. The thermometer should be in a place that will be in the shade all day. You could hang it by a string from a tree branch or lean it against the outside of a window on the north side of your house.

Try to remember to check the air temperature every hour from 8:00 A.M. to 6:00 P.M. Record your measurements on a chart and then make a graph similar to the one with the Boston temperatures (Figure 3-1). At what hour was it warmest? At what hour was it the coolest?

The sun feels hottest about noontime when it is highest in the sky. Yet the warmest time of day is usually about three in the afternoon. Why is this?

Most of the heat in the air does not come directly from the sun. Instead, the air absorbs heat as it comes in contact with the warm ground. The transfer of heat from earth to air continues for a few hours into the afternoon even as the sun feels less hot.

Radiation

The heat of the sun reaches the earth by radiation. When you stand in the sun you can feel its radiant heat warming your body. Investigation 3.2 will enable you to compare how water and soil absorb radiation from the sun.

3.2 Absorption of Radiation Heat by Water and by Soil*

Pack one plastic container with soil and weigh it. Add water to an identical container until it weighs as much as the soil. Keep the containers out of the sun for several hours until the water and soil reach the same temperature. Then place the containers in the sun or under a

Things you'll need:

- two plastic containers of the same size
- soil
- water
- alcohol thermometer

bright light bulb. Measure the temperatures of the soil and water every 10 minutes for at least half an hour. Record the temperature readings on paper. Which heats up more quickly, soil or water?

Next, take the containers out of the heat from the sun or light bulb and continue to measure the temperatures of the soil and water every 10 minutes for another 30 minutes. Which cools off faster, soil or water?

Exploring on Your Own

- Get two shiny, tin cans of the same size. Paint the outside of one can black and allow it to dry. Then half-fill each can with cold water, and place the cans in the sun or near a bright light bulb. After an hour, use a thermometer to check the temperature of the water in each can. In which can has the water temperature increased the most? Could color have affected your results in experiment 3.2? If so, how could you modify the experiment to eliminate any effects due to color?

- You can do another experiment outside to see how color affects the amount of radiant heat absorbed. Find a light-colored car and a dark car parked side by side in the sun. Measure the temperature on each car roof. Which car would be warmer in winter? Why do people in the Middle East wear white robes in the hot desert?

- If you have a magnifying glass, **ask an adult to help you use it to make a fire.** Hold the lens in the sun above a leaf or piece of paper. Move the lens slowly back and forth until the spot of light is as small as possible. Soon the leaf or paper should begin to smoke and catch on fire.

Water, the Great Modifier

Since water holds more heat than other natural substances, the temperatures near oceans and large lakes are less extreme. During the winter, the relatively warm ocean water moderates the air temperatures of coastal cities. The opposite effect occurs in the spring as the sun begins to provide more heat to the earth. Since the ocean waters warm up more slowly, communities near the sea have cooler spring temperatures. The seasons are delayed: the highest temperatures of seashore areas are often in the late summer, and their lowest temperatures come in late winter or early spring.

The graph in Figure 3-2 illustrates the monthly temperatures of two cities in the state of Washington. One city is Seattle, located near the Pacific Ocean. The other city is Spokane, which is about 480 km (300 mi) inland. Is 'City A' Seattle or Spokane? Why does Seattle have milder winters?

Heat Convection

Convection is the motion of liquids or gases because of differences in temperature. Hot water is lighter than the same volume of cold water. Therefore, it tends to rise above the denser, cold water. Convection in gases such as air occurs for the same reason.

The molecules that compose air are in constant motion, and molecules in hot air move faster than molecules in cold air. When

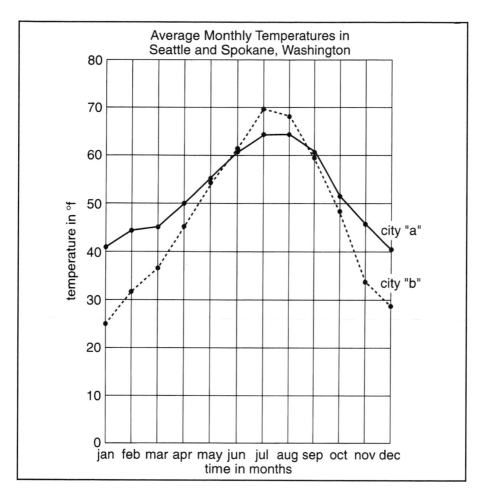

Figure 3-2) Average monthly temperatures in Seattle and Spokane, Washington.

molecules move faster, they take up more space. As air is heated, it expands and becomes lighter. When air is cooled, its molecules slow down, causing it to contract.

Have you ever climbed a mountain? If so, one thing you probably noticed was that it was a lot colder on top. Even in summer, the summits of high mountains are always cold. In the western United States, the tall volcanic peaks of Mt. Rainier, Mt. Hood and Mt. Adams are covered with snow the year-round.

Have you ever wondered why mountain tops are so cold?

Remember, hot air rises. One reason is that as warm air near the ground begins to rise, it expands because the air pressure is less at higher altitudes. When a gas expands, it becomes cooler.

The temperature chart in Figure 3-3 shows monthly temperatures at two weather stations, A and B, in New Hampshire. One station is on the top of Mt. Washington, which is over 1,830 m (6,000 ft) above sea level. The other station is in Concord, a city located at a much lower elevation. Which station is on the mountain top? Which month is the coldest on the mountain?

Exploring on Your Own

- You can see convection in a liquid with a glass baking pan and food coloring. Fill the pan with water and place one end over a stove burner set **on low heat. (Remember, be sure to have permission from an adult before using a stove**.) Immediately add a few drops of food coloring to the water at the cool end of the pan. Look into the water through the side of the glass and watch what happens. You should see the coloring flow down and travel toward the warm end, then rise up and move back toward the cool end. The circulation is caused by convection. What could cause the convection of air masses in the atmosphere?

- See if you can detect the effect of convection in your own room. Place a thermometer on the floor and read the temperature after a few minutes. Now hold the thermometer near the ceiling. Be sure not to touch the thermometer by the bulb or it will measure the temperature of your fingers. Read the temperature after waiting several minutes. Why is the air warmer near the ceiling?

The Seasons

To understand what causes the seasons you must know how Earth moves in space. It is moving in two different ways at the same time.

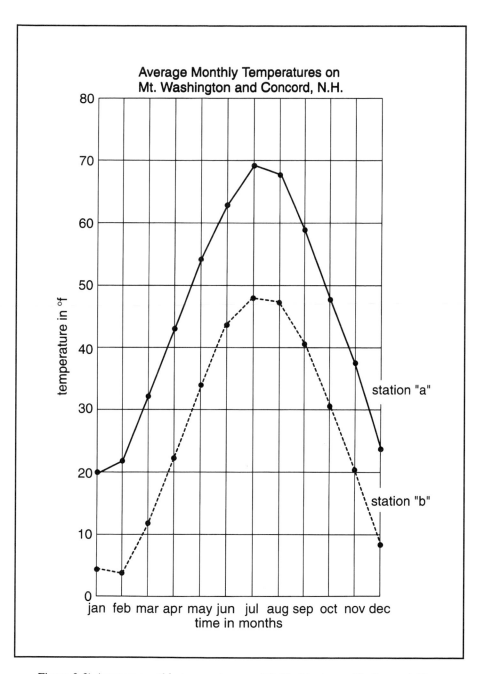

Figure 3-3) Average monthly temperatures on Mt. Washington and in Concord, New Hampshire.

It rotates on its axis as it revolves around the Sun. Earth turns on its axis once every 24 hours, which causes day and night as different sides of Earth face the Sun by day and later face away from the Sun at night.

Earth also is traveling in a huge orbit around the Sun, a journey requiring about 365 days to go around once. Since the axis of Earth is tilted at an angle, its North Pole sometimes is tipped toward the Sun. At other times it is tilted away from the Sun as you can see in Figure 3-4.

If the axis were not tilted, there would be no seasons; every month would be about the same. Why does Earth's tilt cause different seasons? Investigation 3.3 will help you answer this question.

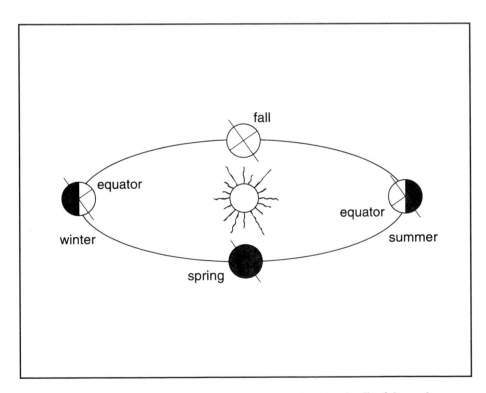

Figure 3-4) The orbit of Earth around the Sun, showing how the tilt of the earth on its axis causes the seasons.

3.3 Cause of the Seasons*

A flashlight will help you to understand how the angle of the sun's rays produces our seasons. Have a friend hold a flashlight about 30 cm (1 ft) above a piece of paper. With a pencil, trace around the circular spot of light. Now ask your friend to hold the flashlight so the light

Things you'll need:

- flashlight
- thermometer
- paper and pencil
- world globe
- small board

hits the paper at an angle. Draw a line around the new oval shape. You can see how the angled light is spread out over a greater area.

You can show the same thing if you have a world globe. Darken the room and have your friend stand close to the globe and shine the flashlight on the United States. To make summertime, pick up the globe and carry it so the axis is tilted toward the flashlight beam. Notice the size of the light spot. Now pick up the globe and move it so the axis is tilting away from the flashlight. What do you notice about the light spot?

From this investigation, you can see that during our warm months of the spring and summer, the North Pole is tipped toward the sun. At these times, the sunlight strikes areas above the equator more directly, providing more heat per area. When the North Pole is tilted away from the sun, the sun's light above the equator is spread out over more surface and so there is less heat for the same area.

With a thermometer you can see how much more heat is provided by direct sunlight. Place a small board so that its surface points toward the sun. Put the thermometer on the board and read the temperature after a few minutes. Next, tilt the board so the sun's rays will strike at an angle. Does the temperature decrease?

If you live where it snows, you might have noticed how the snow sometimes melts faster on sloped banks. The snow on a bank tilted toward the sun, like the one shown in the photograph, receives move direct sunlight than does the snow on level areas.

Latitude

The land and water north of the earth's equator is called the Northern Hemisphere. The Southern Hemisphere lies south of the equator. (See Figure 3-5). Degrees of latitude are measured from the equator, which is taken to be 0°. The North Pole is 90° north latitude; the South Pole is 90° south latitude. What is the latitude where you live?

Inland cities on the same latitude have similar temperatures, except where there are elevation differences or large bodies of water. Cities with latitudes closer to the equator usually have warmer winters

Snow melting on the north bank of a stream.

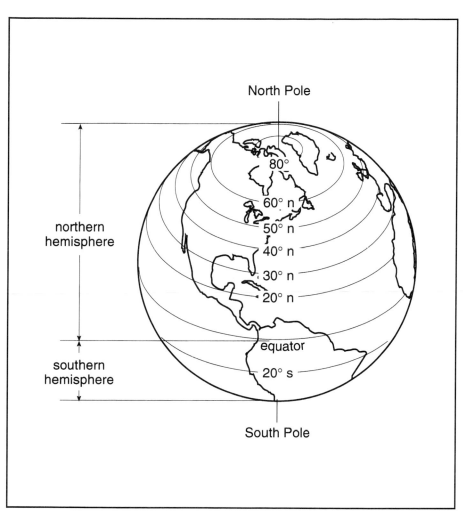

Figure 3-5) The latitudes of the Northern Hemisphere.

than places closer to the poles. In the winter, the heat from the sun's slanting rays is less intense at higher latitudes (latitudes closer to 90°). Also, winter days are shorter as latitude increases. In fact, beyond the arctic and antarctic circles, the sun does not rise at all during part of that hemisphere's winter. And at the poles, darkness prevails throughout the entire winter season.

4

Air and Wind

Normally, we walk around unaware of the fact that we are surrounded by air. It is so thin and light that we walk through it without even sensing its presence. But when you ride your bike or run very fast, you can feel the air moving across your face and body. If you step outdoors on a windy day, you are very much aware of the air pushing on you. You may even be able to hear the wind howling outside your house, school, or library as you read this book.

Weather reports usually include information about the speed and direction of the wind. In Chapter 6 you will learn how to make instruments that will allow you to measure the speed and direction of the wind. Then you will see how you can use this information to make weather forecasts. In this chapter, we will try to find out what makes air move. That is, we will attempt to answer the question: What makes the wind blow?

We will begin with air—the stuff from which winds are made. If air is real, we should be able to weigh it. During investigation 4.1 you will look for evidence that air does have weight.

4.1 Can You Weigh Air?*

Weigh an empty plastic bag and a twist-tie on a balance. Open the bag and pull it through the air to fill it with air. Close the bag, twist the top, and seal it with the twist-tie. Now that the bag is filled with air, weigh it again. Has the weight of the bag and twist-tie changed?

To understand why air appears to be weightless when weighed in air, try this experiment. Use a measuring cup or graduated cylinder to fill a balloon with water as shown in Figure 4-1a. (Use a reasonably large balloon so you can pour 10 mL or more of water into it.) Tie off the neck of the balloon with a twist-tie, being sure that

Things you'll need:

- plastic bags
- twist-ties (tie bands)
- large balloons
- spring balance
- balance that will allow you to detect mass (weight) changes of 0.1 g or less
- thread
- water
- inflatable ball such as soccer ball or football
- air pump and valve to inflate or deflate ball
- measuring cup or graduated cylinder

there are no air bubbles inside the balloon. Attach the water-filled balloon to the spring balance by means of the twist-tie and weigh it again as shown in Figure 4-1b. Finally, lower the water-filled balloon into a jar of water and weigh it once more (Figure 4-1c).

As you can see, an object weighs less in water than it does in air. In fact, as you have also seen, water weighs nothing in water. Water pushes upward on objects with a force that equals the weight of the water displaced (pushed aside) by the object. The buoyant force that the water exerts explains why some objects float in water. When an object that will float is placed in water, it sinks until the buoyant force, the weight of the water displaced, is equal to its weight. Since most people weigh less than an equal volume of water, they float in water. Objects that sink are also buoyed upward, but their weights are greater

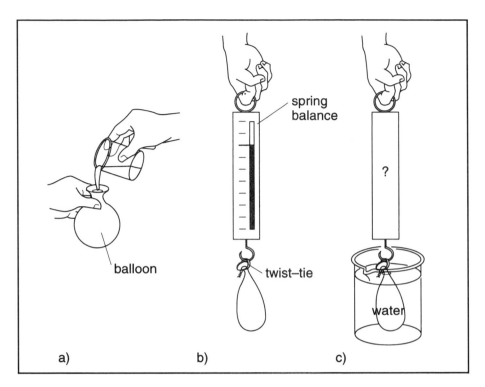

Figure 4-1) Weighing water in water.

than the buoyant force even when they are totally submerged. Still, they weigh less in water, which explains why a stone that you can lift easily in water suddenly feels heavier after it is above the surface.

Since a volume of water is buoyed upward by a force equal to its own weight, water weighs nothing in water. Why do you think air appears to be weightless when weighed in air?

If we could pack more air into a space than it normally holds, that volume would weigh more than it usually does. Take a soccer ball or a football and let all the air out of the ball. Do not squeeze it; just let the air out through a valve until the pressure inside the ball is equal to the air pressure outside the ball. At that point, no more air will come out of the valve.

Weigh the 'empty' ball. Then use a pump and valve to force air into the ball until it is ready for play. Reweigh the ball. How does the weight of the ball with air under pressure compare with the weight of the empty ball? Does air have weight?

Exploring on Your Own

- Does a balloonful of air appear to have weight? How can you find out? How would you weigh a balloonful of helium? What does the behavior of a helium balloon tell you about its weight as compared with the weight of an equal volume of air? How much weight can a helium balloon lift? Does the amount that it can lift depend on the amount of helium in the balloon?

- Put some water in the bottom of a large balloon or a small plastic bag. Seal off the water with a twist-tie. Then place a seltzer tablet in the dry part of the balloon or bag just above the twist-tie. Add a second twist-tie to seal off the top of the bag. Hang the balloon or bag with its seltzer tablet and water on one end of a balance as shown in Figure 4-2. Add weights to the other end of the balance until the beam is level. If you remove the first twist-tie and attach it to the second twist-tie, the total weight of the bag and twist-ties will not change. However, the seltzer tablet will fall into the water and produce carbon dioxide gas. What do you think will happen to the balance? Will the beam stay level, showing no change in weight? Will the side of the beam where the bag or balloon is located go down showing an increase in weight? Or will the weight of the bag and gas appear to decrease? Make your prediction, then test it. Can you explain the result?

Air, Density, and Pressure

Air will move from a region of high pressure to a region of low pressure. It is easy to see that this is true. All you have to do is blow up a balloon. When you open the neck, air will rush out. It moves from the high pressure inside the balloon to the lower pressure outside, creating a miniature wind as it moves. The same thing happens in the atmosphere.

You have seen that air can be compressed and that it weighs more when it is compressed. The pressure of the air (the push it exerts on any given area) in the atmosphere is greater at sea level than it is on a mountain top. The air is squeezed together (compressed) by the weight of the air above it. Since air at sea level is under more air than the air on a mountain top, its pressure is greater. It is more compressed or more closely 'packed together.' A given volume of air at sea level weighs more than the same volume of air on a mountain top.

When one substance has the same mass (or weight) as an equal volume of another substance, we say the two substances have the same

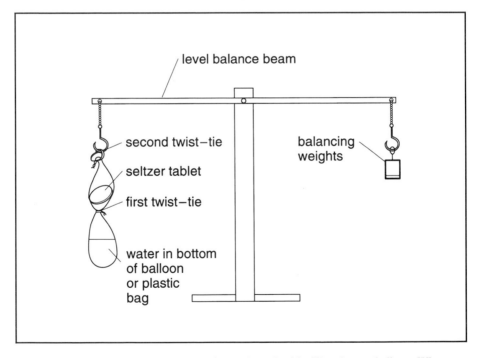

Figure 4-2) Weighing before and after carbon dioxide fills a bag or balloon. What will happen to the balance beam as gas fills the balloon or bag? Will it tip to the right or to the left? Or will it stay level?

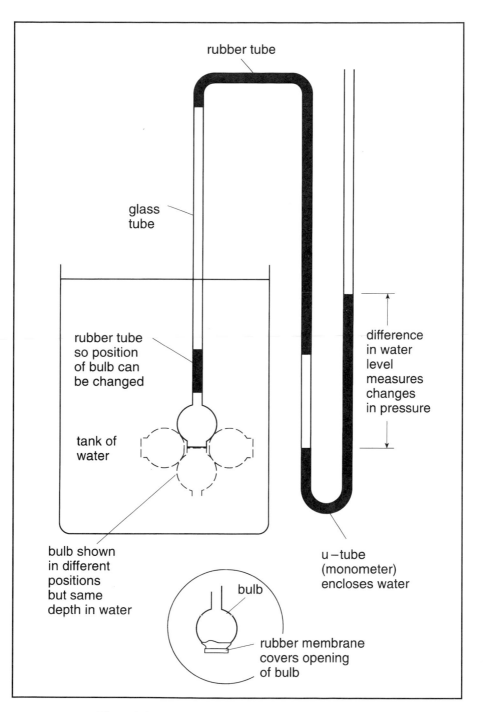

Figure 4-3) Apparatus for measuring changes in pressure.

density. If their volumes are the same and one weighs more than the other, the heavier substance is said to be denser. For example, water is denser than air and mountain air is less dense than sea-level air.

As you read in Chapter 1, Blaise Pascal discovered that air pressure decreases as altitude increases. He also discovered that at any given point in a gas or liquid the pressure is the same in all directions. The manometer shown in Figure 4-3 can be used to measure changes in pressure. (Perhaps you have seen a similar device—a mercury-filled tube called a sphygmomanometer that doctors use to measure your blood pressure.) If someone moves the bulb deeper in the water, the pressure will increase and the water column on the right side of the U-shaped tube will rise as the column on the left side falls. If the person now turns the bulb in any direction, so that the water pushes down, up, or sideways on the bulb's membrane, there is no change in the water levels in the U-tube, as long as the bulb stays at the same depth in the water. The pressure is the same in all directions. With a barometer, you can show that this is true for air pressure as well.

Suppose we have a volume of cold water or cold air and an equal volume of warm water or warm air. Will the equal volumes of water weigh the same? Will the equal volumes of air weigh the same?

Let us look at water first. You can compare the weights of equal volumes of warm and cold water by comparing their buoyancies as explained in investigation 4.2.

4.2 Water—Hot & Cold— Which Weighs More?*

Nearly fill a plastic vial with hot water from the tap. Put some cold water in another vial and add several drops of food coloring to it. Use an eyedropper to remove some of the colored water from the cold-water vial. Now carefully lower the eyedropper into the vial of hot water so that the tip of the eyedrop-

Things you'll need:

- hot water
- cold water
- plastic vials (medicine or pill vials)
- eyedropper or medicine dropper
- food coloring

per is about halfway between the surface and the bottom. Then *very slowly* squeeze the bulb so that the cold water flows gently into the hot water as shown in Figure 4-4. Does cold water rise or sink in hot water? How does the density of cold water compare with the density of hot water?

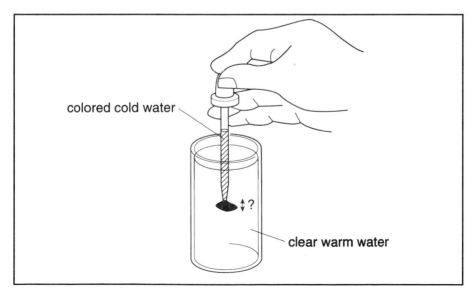

colored cold water

clear warm water

Figure 4-4) Very gently squeeze a drop of colored cold water into a vial of clear, warm water.

Repeat the experiment, but this time add the food coloring to the hot water. Then use the eyedropper to *very gently* squeeze a drop of colored hot water into the center of the clear cold water. Do you expect the colored water to go up or down this time? What do you find when you do the experiment? Was your prediction correct? Is hot water more or less dense than cold water?

Exploring on Your Own

- Fill a balloon with cold tap water as you did during investigation 4.1. Tie off the balloon with a twist-tie. Be sure there are no air bubbles in the balloon. What do you predict will happen if you drop this cold-water balloon into a pail or sink filled with hot tap water? What do you think will happen if you drop a balloon filled with hot tap water into a pail or sink full of cold water? Were your predictions correct?

- To see the effect of air pressure, **ask an adult to help you with this experiment**. Pour about half a cup of water into a one–gallon metal can. Heat the can on a stove or hot plate until the water is boiling. Continue heating the can for several minutes so that the steam drives the air from the can. Then ask the adult to use a pot holder or to wear a glove to remove the can from the heat and quickly seal the opening in the can by screwing on the cap or inserting a rubber stopper. Now watch what happens as the steam in the can cools and condenses. Since the can is sealed, no air can enter the can. But as the steam condenses, there is less and less gas in the can. So as the can cools, how does the gas pressure inside the can compare with the air pressure outside the can? (You can speed up the cooling process by pouring cold water over the can.)

- An air pressure of one atmosphere is approximately equal to a weight of 1 kg per square centimeter or 15 lbs per square inch. Based on the altitude where you live, what is the pressure in your bedroom or classroom (See Figure 1-2)? What is the total force pushing downward on your desk top? Remember, if you are at sea level, the force on *each* square centimeter of your desk top is 1 kg (15 lbs on each square inch). Why does your desk top not collapse under this pressure?

Just for Fun

- The density of air at sea level and room temperature is about 1.2 kg/m^3 or 0.075 lb/ft^3. Using this information, calculate the weight of the air in your bedroom or classroom.

- The atmosphere exerts a pressure equal to that of about 10,000 kg pushing on each square meter or 2,100 lbs on each square foot. The surface area of the earth is approximately 500,000,000,000,000 square meters or 5,400,000,000,000,000 square feet. Find the total weight of the earth's atmosphere in kilograms or pounds.

Air Pressure and Wind

In Chapter 3, you saw how convection currents are set up when water is heated unevenly. From investigation 4.2, you saw that when water is heated, it becomes less dense. Consequently, warm water is buoyed upward by cooler, denser water. You know that liquids expand when heated. All you have to do is watch the alcohol or mercury level in a thermometer. When the thermometer is placed in warm water, the liquid expands and moves up the narrow tube in the thermometer. When it is placed in cold water, the liquid contracts or shrinks and moves down the tube.

Based on what you know about gases, liquids, and density, what do you think will happen to the volume of a gas if it gets warmer? What will happen if it gets colder? During investigation 4.3 you will have a chance to test your predictions.

4.3 Volume of Air and Temperature*

Find an empty plastic soda bottle. Be sure its cap is screwed on tightly so the bottle does not leak. Place the bottle in a freezer. Leave it there for about 10 minutes, and then remove it. What has happened to the bottle? Listen closely as you slowly and silently unscrew the cap. What do you hear? How can you explain what you hear?

Things you'll need:

- narrow-mouth quart or liter plastic soda bottle with screw-on cap

- hot water

- freezer

What happened to the volume of the gas in the bottle when it cooled? Since no gas entered or left the container, what must have happened to the density of the gas as it cooled?

Now remove the bottle's cap and slip a balloon over the mouth of the bottle. Place the bottle in a pan or pail of hot tap water or under a running hot water faucet. What happens to the balloon? What happens to the volume of the air in the bottle as it is heated? What happens to the density of the air as it is heated?

Next, place the bottle and balloon in the freezer. What do you think will happen this time? After about 10 minutes, check your prediction. What happened? Were you right?

Exploring on Your Own

- When a candle burns, it combines with oxygen in the air. But if a candle burns in a jar, will it react with *all* the available oxygen? To find out, use a small piece of clay or melted wax to support a birthday candle in the same shallow dish of water you used in investigation 1.3. **Ask an adult to light the candle and help you with the rest of the experiment.** Light a candle. Wait until it is burning steadily. Then *quickly* lower the tall jar or test tube you used during investigation 1.3 down over the candle as shown in Figure

4-5. How long does the candle burn before it goes out? What happens to the water level in the jar after the candle goes out?

- Do you think water came into the jar because the burning candle used up all the oxygen in the jar? Or did it rise because the air, which had been heated by the candle, cooled and contracted after the candle went out?

- To see that the air does indeed expand when heated by the candle, repeat the experiment **with help from an adult.** But this time stir a drop or two of liquid soap into the colored water in the shallow dish. If the gas does expand, it should produce bubbles when it expands out through the bottom of the jar. Again, *quickly* cover the

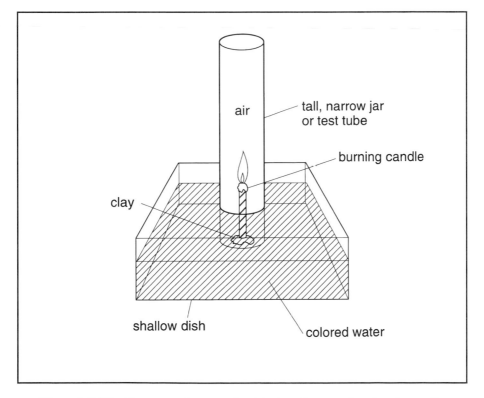

Figure 4-5) What happens to the water level in the tall, narrow jar when the candle goes out?

burning candle with the jar. Do you see any bubbles after you place the jar over the burning candle? Does the air expand when heated?

- Repeat the experiment, but before you do, place a piece of steel wool that has been soaked in vinegar at the bottom of the jar or tube. What do you predict will happen to the water level in the jar if you leave the jar overnight? Try it! Were you right?

- You see now that water and air behave the same way when heated or cooled. Consequently, warm air is less dense than cold air, just as warm water is less dense than cold water. As a result, cold air exerts a greater pressure than an equal volume of warm air. Cold air will flow under warm air and set up convection currents similar to the convection currents you saw in water in Chapter 3. It is cold, dense air moving into a fireplace that buoys warm air and the smoke up the chimney. It is dense, high pressure air that pushes under less dense, low pressure air creating a motion of air that we call wind.

Exploring on Your Own

- Open a freezer door and place your arm beneath the opening into the freezer. Then hold your arm above the opening. Why does your arm feel much colder under the opening than it does above the opening?

- In the summer, when there is a screen door outside an entrance door, it is easy to close the door. Why is it so much harder to close the same door in the winter when a closed storm door is present?

Local Winds

If you are sitting on the beach by the ocean on a warm summer afternoon, you will probably feel a breeze blowing in from the ocean. As you saw in Chapter 3, land heats up a lot faster than a large body of water; therefore, the land near the ocean warms faster than the water. As a result, the air over the land will expand becoming less dense than the air over the ocean. The cooler, denser air over the water will flow under the warmer air over the land creating an on-shore breeze as shown in Figure 4-6a. At night, the land will cool faster than the ocean. This often causes an off-shore breeze (Figure 4-6b).

Similar effects occur as air over the dark soil of plowed fields warms faster than the air above grassy meadows or tree-filled forests. Air over mountains tends to cool faster at night than air over valleys. This creates cool, down-slope breezes, while opposite effects occur

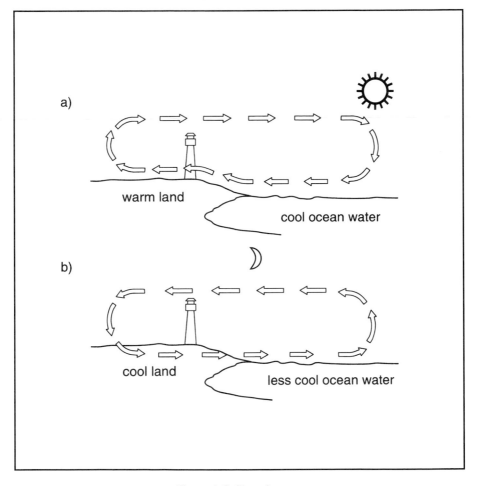

Figure 4-6) Shore breezes.

during the daytime as mountain air warms faster than air at lower altitudes.

Winds Across the Earth

In Figure 4-7 you see a general view of the earth's major wind flow patterns in the Northern Hemisphere. Based on these patterns you might think that the flow of air from high pressure to low pressure can explain all the earth's winds. But actually the movement of air over great distances is more complicated because the earth turns on its axis. Investigation 4.4 will help you to understand how the earth's rotation affects the movement of air.

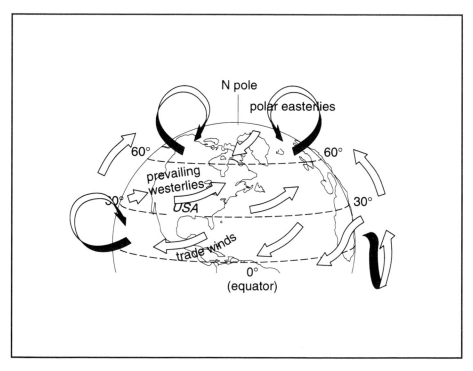

Figure 4-7) General air movement (wind) in the Northern Hemisphere.

4.4 Motion on a Rotating Surface*

Starting at the upper right hand corner of a sheet of paper, make a line by moving a pencil straight down the sheet at a slow steady speed. As you do so, have a friend pull the paper slowly to the right. What happens to the shape of the line on the paper? Repeat the experiment, but this time have your friend pull the paper to the right slowly at first and then with increasing speed. What is the shape of the line this time?

Things you'll need:

- turntable, "lazy Susan," or piano stool
- paper
- pencil
- tape
- ruler
- old record or circular sheet of cardboard
- marking pen
- scissors

To see how this is related to the flow of air across the earth's surface, tape a sheet of paper to an old record and place it on a turntable. The paper should be cut to match the shape of the record. Alternatively, you can tape the record to a "lazy Susan" or a piano stool and have someone spin the "lazy Susan" or piano stool by hand in the same direction that a record would spin. If you don't have an old record, you can use a circular sheet of cardboard. Let the center of the circle represent the North Pole. The circumference of the circle represents the earth's equator. With the record or cardboard circle rotating, use a marking pen to draw a straight line from the center of the circle (North Pole) to the edge (equator).

Stop the motion of the record and look at what you have drawn. If you doubt that you really drew a straight line, hold a ruler beside the pen just above the record to guide the pen as you draw the line. Notice how the "easterly" rotation of the record or cardboard (earth) causes the line to curve to the right.

Repeat the experiment, but this time draw a straight line from the edge (Equator) of the circle to the center (North Pole). Again, you will see that the line is curved and seems to bend to the right. Why do the straight lines that you drew appear as curved lines on the rotating record or cardboard?

Here are some things to do and some hints that may help you to answer that question. Using the same apparatus, make a circle on the turning record or cardboard without moving the marking pen. How did you do this? Where would you place the pen on the circle so that it would make only a point as the table turned? How can you use two pens to make two circles, one larger than the other? Under which pen was the surface (earth) moving faster?

How far does a point at the center of the rotating circle (North Pole) move in one revolution? How fast does it move? Look at a point halfway between the center and the rim of the circle (latitude 45°). How far does it move in one revolution? What is its speed? Which points on the circle (earth) move fastest? Finally, why do the straight lines that you drew on the rotating circle appear as curved lines on the rotating record or cardboard?

Winds moving across the earth's Northern Hemisphere appear to shift to the right just as the pencil did when you pulled it in a straight line across the rotating disk. Suppose a cold mass of air begins moving southward from the North Pole into a warmer, less dense air mass to the south. Its eastward velocity at the pole is zero. But as it moves southward, the earth's eastward speed increases. Since the air moving southward has no eastward velocity, it seems to be moving westward (to the right of its path) to people on the earth who are moving more rapidly eastward than the air (Figure 4-8).

You see or feel a similar effect when you ride your bike on a calm (windless) day. To you, it seems as if a wind is blowing into your face because you are moving into still air. On the other hand, if you ride southward at 16 kmph (10 mph) when there is a 16 kmph (10 mph) north wind, you feel no wind. From your point of view, the wind speed is zero.

For similar reasons, winds blowing northward in the Northern Hemisphere appear to be shifted eastward (to the right) because they have a larger eastward velocity than do points on the earth to the north of the air mass.

Water currents in the ocean, such as the Gulf Stream that flows northward from the Gulf of Mexico, are also bent due to the earth's rotation. The shift of winds and ocean currents to the right of their path in the Northern Hemisphere (to the left in the Southern Hemisphere) as a result of the earth's rotation is called the *Coriolis effect*.

Look again at Figure 4-7. It shows air that has been heated by the sun rising near the equator and moving northward. It is shifted eastward as it flows by the earth's rotation. At about 30°N latitude, the large masses of air moving northeastward pile up creating a high pressure region. This forces some of the air downward. Near the

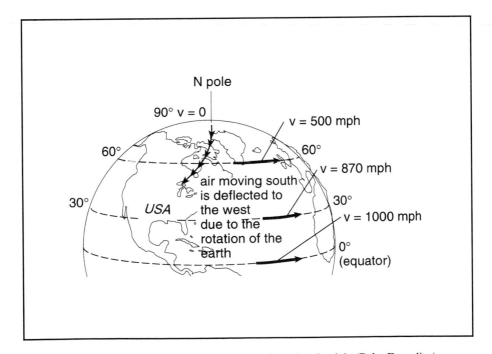

Figure 4-8) Arctic air moving southward is deflected to the right (Polar Easterlies) as a result of the earth's rotation. This is known as the Coriolis effect. Notice how the velocity of the earth due to rotation decreases as you move northward from the equator.

earth's surface, this air flows southward turning right (westward) as it goes, creating the trade winds that blow from the northeast.

Some of the air that piles up at 30°N latitude flows northward and is deflected to the east by the Coriolis effect. These winds constitute the prevailing westerlies that move over the middle latitudes.

Not all the air sinks downward at 30°N latitude; some of it continues northward high above the earth cooling by radiation as it moves. Having cooled, it is denser and sinks back to the earth near the poles.

This dense, high pressure, polar air now moves southward replacing warmer air. It is deflected to the right (westward) as it moves, producing winds known as the polar easterlies that blow from the northeast. At about 60°N latitude, these winds collide with the prevailing westerlies from the southwest. The cold, polar air pushes under the warmer westerlies forcing the warmer air upward. The rising warm air expands at higher altitudes where the pressure is less. This expansion gives rise to cooling just as air from an air hose cools when it is allowed to expand. If there is sufficient water vapor in the air, it will condense forming the precipitation so common in the middle latitudes. Occasionally, the cold air will push through the warmer air giving rise to cold waves that may extend as far southward as 30°N latitude.

Exploring on Your Own

- Look closely at the lines you drew on the rotating circle in project 4.4. Where are the lines blurred the most? Why?

- Why are people allowed to walk on a merry-go-round while it is at rest but not while it is moving?

Just for Fun

- From what you learned during project 4.4, see if you can move the pen so as to draw a line from the center to the edge of the circle that really is straight. How can you draw a line that really is straight on the rotating circle when you move the pen from the edge to the center? Then draw a line all the way across the rotating circle that appears to be straight when the rotation stops.

- Take a ride on a merry-go-round. Sit or stand where you will get the fastest ride. Sit or stand where you will get the slowest ride.

The Jet Stream

The jet stream was discovered by United States Air Force pilots during World War II. Flying over the Pacific Ocean near Japan they consistently reported west winds of about 160 kmph (100 mph) at altitudes of 6-12 km (20,000-40,000 ft). The height of the tropopause (See Figure 1-2), which is higher near the equator than near the poles, does not change gradually. It changes dramatically, as does its temperature, and it is in these regions, at latitudes of about 30°N and 45°N, that jet streams arise. These fast moving air streams have peak speeds of about 230 kmph (140 mph). They are about 500 km (300 mi) wide and move from west to east at altitudes of 6-12 km (4-8 mi). Airplanes flying from west to east often fly at the same altitude and latitude as the jet stream to take advantage of the strong tailwind it provides.

These jet streams sometimes extend around the world with winds high enough to carry air around the world in five days. They give rise to low pressure regions where storms develop. Thus, southward and northward shifts of the jet stream are accompanied by similar shifts of storm tracks and the weather associated with them. When a jet stream moves closer to the equator than normal, the shift is usually accompanied by lower temperatures and increased precipitation. The jet stream in the middle latitudes, coupled with the prevailing westerlies, is the reason most of our weather comes from the west. Normally, we can figure it will take about three days for a weather system to move across the United States.

The Coriolis Effect, Pressure Differences, Friction, and Wind

Air tends to move from high pressure to low pressure, but it is diverted to the right by the Coriolis effect. Near the surface of the earth there is another force that affects the wind's speed and direction—friction! If you try to slide a box across the floor, friction between the box and the floor pushes against the box and slows it down. In a similar way, air is slowed down by the frictional forces between it and the trees, grass, and buildings over which it moves.

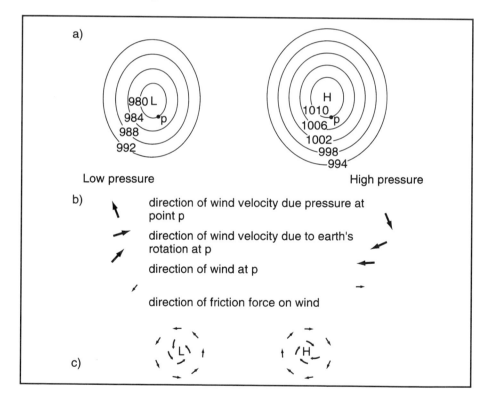

Figure 4-9 a) Isobars are lines marking equal pressures around high pressure centers (H) and low pressure centers (L). 4-9b) As a result of forces due to pressure, friction, and the earth's rotation, winds tend to move parallel to isobars rather than perpendicular to them. 4-9c) Wind direction at a number of points around H and L.

As a result of these forces, the actual direction of winds tends to be along *isobars* rather than directly from a region of high pressure to one of low pressure. Isobars are drawn by meteorologists to map positions of equal pressure. The value of the pressure, in millibars (mb), is written on each isobar. (A millibar is a pressure equal to one-thousandth the pressure of the atmosphere at sea level.) Where the lines are close together, the pressure changes rapidly and so the wind speeds are high. As you can see from Figure 4-9a, the isobar lines surround a high pressure or low pressure and are separated by pressure differences of 4 mb. Figure 4-9b shows you how the Coriolis effect, air pressure, and friction cause winds to blow along isobars rather than directly from high pressure to low pressure.

Buys Ballot's Rule says that if you stand with your back to the wind, high pressure will be on your right and low pressure on your left. Using Figure 4-9c, show that this rule is correct. From Figure 4-9, you can see that in the Northern Hemisphere winds blow counterclockwise around low pressure centers or cyclones (as viewed from above) and clockwise around high pressure (anticyclones).

Winds are a very important part of our weather. They carry clouds that bring needed rain to end a drought. They bring welcome relief from scorching heat and high humidity. The energy in moving winds can be used to turn windmills that generate electricity, pump water, and do other kinds of useful work. However, under certain conditions, air pressure can change very rapidly from one place to another. When this happens, winds can become so strong that they blow down trees and buildings. You will investigate such violent winds in Chapter 5.

5

Stormy Weather

You have seen how water vapor condenses to rain and snow in clouds and falls back to earth. Sometimes rain is accompanied by thunder and lightning and very strong winds. In this chapter we will explore the severe weather that we find in thunderstorms, tornadoes, and hurricanes.

Thunderstorms

A thunderstorm is one of nature's most feared displays of unpredictable power. The storm's arrival is signaled by a monstrous cloud that quickly grows and towers above the surrounding clouds. The sky darkens as turbulent wind gusts pound against trees and houses. Soon comes the downpour of rain, perhaps mixing with a bombardment of hailstones. The storm's passage is punctuated by brilliant flashes of lightning and deafening claps of thunder. Then, almost as quickly as it began, the rain ceases and the sky begins to clear.

Thunderstorm Development

A thunderstorm is born when warm, humid air rises and cools, causing the water vapor to condense into a cumulus cloud. At first, the cloud expands upwards for only a short distance before dissipating, because the cloud droplets evaporate as they become mixed with the surrounding drier air. However, after the water drops evaporate, the air is moister, so the rising air is able to condense at successively higher levels. As the cumulus cloud grows taller, it often takes the shape of a rising dome or anvil.

The cloud continues to build as long as it is fed by rising air from below. At first, the strong updrafts prevent any precipitation from falling. But as the cloud reaches well above the freezing level, its water droplets grow larger. Eventually the rising air can no longer keep them suspended, and rain begins to fall amid lightning and thunder. Sometimes in the dry air over a desert, the raindrops from a thunderstorm evaporate before they reach the ground.

Thunderstorms do not last very long. The storm's precipitation produces strong downdrafts that eliminate the humid updrafts, thereby cutting off the needed 'fuel' supply. The storm destroys itself.

Thunderstorm Distribution

Meteorologists estimate that at any given time, there are 1,000 to 2,000 thunderstorms occurring throughout the world. The map in Figure 5-1 shows the frequency of storms in the United States. Thunderstorms, which almost always occur on hot summer days, are most common in the southeastern United States along the Gulf Coast and in the southern Rocky Mountains. Thunderstorms are rare along the West Coast because the temperature differences between the land and water are not as great.

Rain from thunderstorms is useful in providing the earth with water during the dry summer months. In addition, the storms often bring welcome cooling during uncomfortably hot days. The blast of refreshing air from the downdraft can lower the air temperature as much as 10°C (18°F) in just a few minutes. Unfortunately, the temperature usually rises again soon after the storm passes.

Thunder and Lightning

Lightning is a giant spark. For lightning to occur, large concentrations of opposite charges must exist within a cloud. For reasons not well understood, the top of a thunderstorm cloud becomes positively charged and the lower portion becomes negatively charged. The first lightning strokes are within the cloud. Lightning to the ground starts with a thin 'leader' stroke from the cloud followed by a much stronger

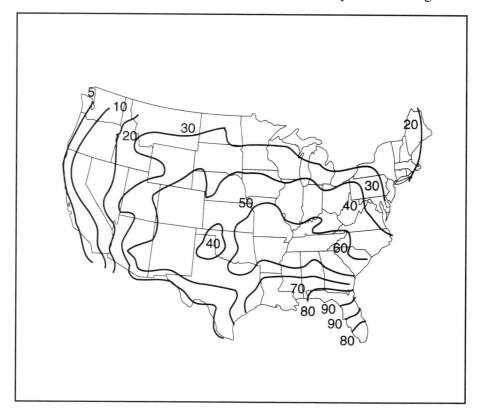

Figure 5-1) Thunderstorm distribution: the numbers show the average number of thunderstorms during the year in the United States.

Lightning flash, with forks and branches traced through the surrounding clouds.

'return' stroke back from the ground to the cloud. A single lightning bolt oscillates back and forth many times in less than a second. The energy in a large thunderstorm is far greater than the energy released by a nuclear bomb.

Thunder occurs because the air around the lightning bolt becomes heated to temperatures as high as 30,000°C (54,000°F). The heated air expands suddenly and creates a sound wave. On a much smaller scale, it is expanding air that makes the pop when a balloon breaks.

5.1 How Far Away is the Storm?

You can estimate the distance to a thunderstorm by measuring the time it takes the sound of the thunder to reach you. When you see a lightning flash, begin counting seconds. Count slowly, perhaps saying to yourself, "One thousand one, one thousand two," and so on. Continue to count until you hear the thunder. If the time is five seconds, the storm is about 1.6 km (1 mi) away.

Do not go outside even if a thunderstorm seems far away. Estimate the distance to the storm from inside your house where it is safer.

Light and sound travel at different speeds. Since light travels at 298,800 km (186,000 mi) a second, you see the lightning almost the instant it occurs. But sound travels much more slowly, only about 340 m (1,100 ft) a second, or 1.6 km (1 mi.) in five seconds. How far away was the lightning if you see the lightning and then hear the thunder after counting to three? Write a rule that will allow you to estimate the distance to any thunderstorm.

Thunderstorm Damage

Downdrafts from severe thunderstorms may have caused several airplane crashes. In 1975, a jet above New York City's Kennedy Airport apparently flew directly into the center of a strong downdraft. Suddenly it lost altitude and crashed on the runway.

Sometimes excessive rain from a thunderstorm causes flash floods. Roads are inundated and farm fields eroded. Trees and crops can be damaged by driving wind, raindrops, and hailstones.

Thunderstorm lightning causes even more destruction. When a tree is struck by lightning, the moisture in the wood is suddenly vaporized, and the bark might be blown off. If too much of the bark is shattered, the tree will die. Sometimes the lightning bolt creates so much heat that the tree will be set on fire. Lightning starts about 9,000 fires each year in the United States.

To reduce the risk of lightning fires in houses and other buildings, lightning rods are mounted along the highest parts of a building's roof. The rods are connected by cables to a metal strip buried in the ground. If lightning does strike, the electric charges will be carried harmlessly into the ground.

Thunderstorm Safety

More than 100 people in the United States are killed by lightning each year. Many of these deaths would not occur if the victims would follow safety procedures. The safest place to be during a thunderstorm is inside a house or car. The approach of a storm can almost always be detected by the towering cumulus clouds or the sound of distant thunder rumblings. Take shelter before the storm arrives; do not wait until it begins to rain. Avoid open fields where you might be the tallest object below a thunder cloud.

While inside your house during the storm, do not use a water faucet, telephone, television set, or any other electrical appliance. Do not hold or be near anything that is metal.

If you are caught outside during a storm, do not hide under a tree that stands alone. Since lightning tends to strike tall structures, you would be safer in an open field. Try to find a ditch or low place, and keep your head low by crouching down. You should not lie on the ground, however.

Lightning is dangerous; never take any chances in a thunderstorm!

Tornadoes

Imagine you are listening to a radio in your room, when you hear your terrified mother shout, "Tornado!" A killer storm has been spotted. You have been taught what to do: huddle near a basement wall. Soon you hear a shrill whistle and awful rumbling. Never have you heard such a loud noise! The whole house is shaking violently. Suddenly it gets

A tornado, showing the typical funnel shape.

brighter. You look up the stairs and see that the roof has been blown away. Even though the roaring has stopped, you are too scared to move.

Tornadoes are rapidly rotating winds that blow around a small area of extreme low pressure. The thin funnel cloud, seen clearly in the photograph, may extend to the ground. It rotates in a counterclockwise direction when viewed from above. The funnel cloud usually picks up dust and debris which makes its tip appear dark and ominous.

Although twisters are a very powerful kind of storm, they are usually small in size. The diameter of the funnel tube is only 91-183 m (100-200 yds) wide. Most tornadoes move at a speed of about 32-64 kmph (20-40 mph), and last for only a few minutes. The whirling winds near the center, or vortex, of the funnel often exceed 480 kmph (300 mph).

Tornadoes occur in many parts of the world. The United States averages more than 700 tornadoes yearly, more than any other country. Although there have been tornadoes in every state, the greatest number are in the 'tornado belt' of the central plains. Oklahoma, Texas, and Kansas are the states that have the most. Tornadoes are most common in the spring when warm surface air is present. They occur at all times of the day and night, but are most frequent in the late afternoon when the surface air is unstable with cooler air above warm air.

5.2 Make a Liquid Tornado

You can make a liquid tornado with two plastic soda bottles. The best size to use are those with a volume of 0.5 or 1 liter. Fill one bottle about three–fourths full with water, and add a few drops of food coloring. Tape the mouths of the bottles to-

Things you'll need:

- two plastic soda bottles
- water
- food coloring
- masking tape

gether with a long strip of masking tape as shown in Figure 5-2.

To make the tornado, turn over the joined bottles so the one with water is on top. Immediately swirl the bottles around for about 5 seconds, and then place them on a table. As the water drains into the lower bottle, a spinning whirlpool should form. Does your liquid volcano twist clockwise or counterclockwise? How can you make one that turns in the other direction?

Just for Fun

- You can make tornado-like air rings with a one-gallon plastic milk carton. (See Figure 5-3). Aim the opening at a friend, and slap the bottom of the carton with your fingers. If you aim right, an invisible air ring will blow your friend's hair. How far can you make an air ring travel? **Ask an adult to help you try to blow out a burning candle** with your air gun.

Tornado Formation

Tornadoes tend to form with severe thunderstorms when the air is unstable. A wedge of cold, dry air flows above a mass of warm and humid air near the ground. As the jet stream carries away the upper air, air from below is drawn up to replace it. The atmosphere is unstable because the warm air continues to rise from the ground: a condition that often leads to the development of severe thunderstorms.

The first sign that a tornado might form from a thunderstorm is rotating clouds that bulge from the base of the storm. If the rotating clouds continue to lower, a thin funnel forms within the cloud wall and extends toward the ground. Occasionally, several funnels stretch from a single storm cloud. The destructive tip may bob up and down, skipping some places and causing devastation in others.

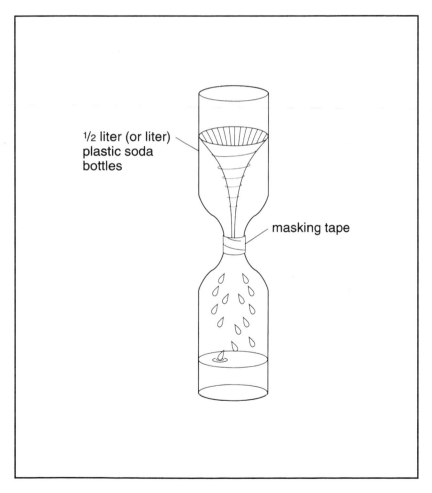

Figure 5-2) How to make a liquid tornado with two soda bottles.

Figure 5-3) Slapping the bottom of a plastic milk jug creates powerful air rings.

Tornado Damage

The intense winds of a twister destroy buildings and upset cars and trucks. The extremely low air pressure in the vortex can cause closed-up houses and barns to explode when the normal pressure of air inside pushes outward.

Another destructive force in a tornado is the strong updraft at the center of the funnel. Houses, animals, cars, and people can be picked up and carried hundreds of meters through the air. Often people picked up by a tornado updraft are killed when they are dropped suddenly. Yet sometimes, people in an updraft have been set down gently without injury. Once a railroad car with 117 passengers was lifted and dumped in a ditch 8 m (25 ft) away.

Tornadoes have caused some strange things to happen. Frogs and fish have fallen with rain following a tornado. The animals were lifted from nearby ponds and carried with the storm. Several times people have seen 'blood rain' which occurs when a tornado picks up red clay and mixes it with the rain.

Just for Fun

- You can see the force of air pressure with a test tube fitted with a one–hole stopper and glass tube. **With adult help,** boil some water in the test tube in order to drive out most of the air. Then quickly invert the test tube and hold the end of the tube in a glass of water as shown in Figure 5-4. Air pressure should drive the water up the glass tube until the test tube is almost filled with water.

Tornado Safety

Of course, it is very important for people to know when a tornado is

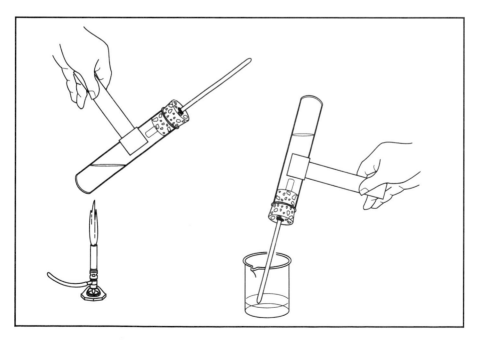

Figure 5-4) Air pressure pushes water into the test tube after most of the air is driven out by heating.

approaching. When there is violent thunderstorm activity, the National Severe Storms Forecast Center in Kansas City, Missouri, will issue a 'tornado watch.' Many communities have trained volunteers to look for developing tornado funnels. Once a tornado is spotted, a 'tornado warning' is issued by the local weather service office. In some towns, sirens will sound to alert people to the approaching storm. Radio and television stations interrupt their programs to broadcast warnings.

More recently, radar has been useful in detecting tornadoes. Reflected radar waves bouncing off raindrops produce white areas on the radar screen. An unusual hook-shaped echo often appears when a tornado is forming from a thunderstorm.

If a tornado begins when you are at home, you should open some windows a little and get away from them. Air can escape from the house through the open windows and equalize the pressure. Go into your storm cellar if you have one. If not, crouch under a workbench in the cellar, under a staircase, or under your bed.

If you are away from home in a tornado, get off the street. If you can, go into a building, but keep away from windows and doors. If you are not near a building, lie flat on the ground and cover your head with your arms. In school, go to an inside wall on the lowest floor, crouch down, and cover your head.

Waterspouts and Dust Devils

A waterspout is formed when a tornado passes over a large body of water. The winds in a waterspout are not as strong as regular tornado winds. Also, unlike tornadoes, waterspouts can be generated in the absence of thunderstorms. Waterspouts are common over the warm waters of the Florida Keys, where almost one hundred occur each month during the summer. A waterspout does not draw water up into the core of its funnel.

Have you ever noticed a swirling column of dust on a hot day? These are nicknamed dust devils or whirlwinds. The miniature tornado is created when hot air rises and is replaced by the surrounding air that rushes in with a swirling motion. A dust devil can rotate in either direction.

Hurricanes

Hurricanes are gigantic storms that are born over tropical oceans. Their winds often exceed 240 kmph (150 mph) and cover an area 640 km (400 mi) across. Hurricane clouds in the Northern Hemisphere spiral in a counterclockwise direction toward the eye at the storm's center. Within the eye, the winds are light and the sky is often clear. Surrounding the eye is the eye wall, a ring of intense thunderstorms that extend upward to a height of 16 km (10 mi).

Hurricanes have different names in other parts of the world. In the Pacific near the Phillipine Islands, a hurricane is called a typhoon. In the Indian Ocean, it is a cyclone, and in Australia, it is called a willy willy.

Most of the hurricanes that affect the United States begin as a mass of thunderstorms in the Atlantic Ocean near the bulging west coast of Africa. If the winds increase to over 118 kmph (74 mph) as the storm moves west, it is classified as a hurricane. Many Atlantic hurricanes strike the islands of the West Indies in the Caribbean and continue into the Gulf of Mexico. Other times the hurricane will loop to the north and travel up the East Coast as far as Maine. The less frequent hurricanes that occur in the Pacific off the Mexican Coast occasionally reach California.

The hurricane season extends from June into November, but they are most frequent from August through October.

Hurricane Formation

Hurricanes form over tropical oceans where the winds are light and the surface temperature of the water is uniform over a large area. At first, the future hurricane is just a mass of unorganized thunderstorms.

The eye of a hurricane.

As the surface winds converge, the Coriolis effect (Chapter 4) causes the air to start to spin in a counterclockwise motion in the Northern Hemisphere. The rotation pushes air toward the center, forcing hot, moist air to rise. As the rising moisture condenses, heat is produced and further warms the rotating air. A chain reaction takes place. As more and more moist tropical air sweeps in to replace the rising air, there is more and more condensation. This makes the air inside the storm rise faster and faster until a hurricane is born.

A hurricane can last two to three weeks if it remains over warm water. It will weaken rapidly, however, as it travels over colder water or land. In order to sustain its strength, a hurricane requires the energy released from rising warm, moist air.

Hurricane Damage

A hurricane's strong winds generate large waves, sometimes 9 to 14 m (30 to 45 ft) high. The swells from the waves move ahead of the storm and reach distant beaches days before the hurricane arrives.

The high winds also produce something known as the storm surge. The surge is caused by a bulge in the ocean that forms under the low air pressure area in the storm. The level of the seawater in a storm surge can rise as much as 6 m (20 ft). Most of a hurricane's damage is caused by coastal flooding, which is especially severe if the surge and huge waves arrive at high tide.

The heavy rains that accompany a hurricane might drop as much a 0.6 m (2 ft) of water in 24 hours. Even after the storm moves inland, torrential rains can fill rivers until they overflow.

In 1900, a hurricane completely flooded the gulf city of Galveston, Texas. More than 6,000 people died. Important hurricanes in recent years were Camille, which struck Mississippi in 1969, Hugo, which ravaged Charleston, South Carolina in 1989, and Andrew, which swept across south Florida in 1992. The worst hurricane of all times was the 1970 killer cyclone that flooded the coast of Bangladesh and took more than 250,000 lives.

Hurricane Warning and Safety

Meteorologists study images from weather satellites to see if any cloud formations are developing into the pinwheel shape that is characteristic of a hurricane. The formation is designated a tropical storm when its winds reach 62 kmph (39 mph) and a hurricane when the winds reach 118 kmph (74 mph).

Each year, hurricanes are designated by names in alphabetical order. The names alternate between female names and male names. Do you know if your name was ever assigned to a hurricane?

Special airplanes, equipped with radar and weather instruments, fly through hurricanes to measure temperature, air pressure, and wind speed. They even fly into the eye of the hurricane in order to plot the exact position of the storm.

The Weather Bureau issues a hurricane warning when forecasters think the storm will reach land within 24 hours. This gives time for people who live in low areas near the sea to evacuate inland before the storm arrives. Ships at sea try to change course and avoid the storm.

If a hurricane warning is issued for your town or city, you should prepare for the storm immediately. Store clean water in your bathtub and in jugs. Since you may lose electric power, be sure you have a flashlight with fresh batteries and a portable radio so you can hear weather bulletins and emergency information. Board up large windows with plywood and criss–cross smaller windows with masking tape to reduce the danger from flying glass.

Do not go outside during a hurricane. You could be hit by a falling tree or by debris picked up by the fierce winds. Even if it clears, do not go out right away. You may be in the eye of the storm, and more wind and rain could arrive soon.

6

Your Weather Station

Perhaps the best way for you to learn about the weather is to make your own weather station. With weather instruments, you can measure air temperature, air pressure, humidity, rainfall, wind direction, and wind speed. By studying your daily observations, you might be able to make weather predictions.

There are thousands of official weather stations throughout the United States. Because accurate weather conditions and forecasts are vital for safe airplane travel, every airport has its own weather station. Weather information from these and other stations around the country is collected by regional National Weather Service offices.

The instruments you should have for your weather station are a thermometer, a wind vane, an anemometer, a rain gauge, a barometer, and a hygrometer. Most of the instruments used by national weather stations are complicated and expensive. For your weather station, you can make some of the instruments yourself and buy others that do not cost too much.

Thermometer

You already know about one of the most important weather instruments: the thermometer. You probably have at least one thermometer inside your house on the thermostat that regulates the temperatures in your home. You also might have another thermometer mounted outside your house. If not, you could buy a thermometer at a hardware store.

Outside air temperature readings should be made in the shade, since a thermometer in the sun will show a temperature higher than the true temperature of the air. You could hang your thermometer on the north side of your house where it will be out of the sun all day. Or you could find a shady place on the trunk of a large tree.

Thermometers at many weather stations are placed inside a large white box. The shelter has slotted openings for air but not sunlight.

Measuring Wind Direction and Wind Speed

To find the direction from which the wind is blowing you will need a wind vane, sometimes called a weather vane. Investigation 6.1 will show you how to make such an instrument. To find the wind's speed you'll need an anemometer, which you can make in investigation 6.2.

6.1 Make a Wind Vane*

A wind vane shows the direction of the wind. It tells where it is blowing from, not the direction it is blowing toward. You probably have seen wind vanes attached to the top of barn roofs and church steeples. Small airports have large wind vanes, called wind socks, to show pilots the wind direction when they take off or land in their airplanes. A smaller cloth streamer often is mounted on the top of goalposts on

Things you'll need:

- 15 cm x 40 cm (6 in x 16 in) plywood, 1/2 in thick

- long, thin screw and washer

- drill and bit

- coping saw or jigsaw

- 2 x 4 posts 1.7 m (5.5 ft) long

- magnetic compass

a football field. It is important for the kicker to know the direction of the wind when a field goal is kicked.

Ask an adult to help you cut a large arrow from a piece of plywood. Move the arrow back and forth on your finger until you find its balance point. Drill a hole through the arrow at this spot, using a drill bit that is slightly larger than the screw you will use to attach the wind vane to the post. The washer between the post and the wind vane allows it to spin easier. (See Figure 6-1).

Your wind vane should be mounted on a wooden post about 1.2 m (4 ft) tall. Since the wind's direction is often changed as it blows around trees or buildings, the post should be out in the open. Bury the bottom end of the post in a hole about 46 cm (18 in) deep.

In order to find directions, you will need a compass. Hold the compass level and twist it around until 'north' on the face is pointing in the same direction as the marked end of the needle. The main points of the compass are north (N), south (S), east (E), and west (W). In between these are northeast (NE), southeast (SE), southwest (SW), and northwest (NW).

On some days the wind might not be strong enough to move the wind vane. But when there is at least a moderate breeze, your wind vane should point in the direction from which the wind is blowing.

Exploring on Your Own

- In most places, the compass needle does not point directly north. You can find true north by watching the sun's shadow. Push a pencil straight into the ground on a sunny day. Beginning at 11:00 in the morning, measure the length of the shadow with a ruler. Sometime between 11:00 A.M. and 2:00 P.M., the shadow will be the shortest. When it is, the shadow will point toward true north.

- Using your wind vane, design an experiment to find out what the prevailing wind is where you live. Does it vary from season to season?

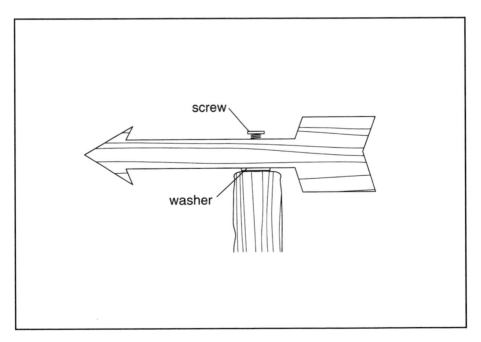

Figure 6-1) Plans for a wooden wind vane.

6.2 Make an Anemometer*

An anemometer is an instrument for measuring the speed of the wind. The anemometer used at weather stations has three cups which catch the wind and rotate. There is a small generator at the base of the shaft which sends an electric current to the meter dial in the station.

You can make another kind of anemometer from a small piece of wood about 15 cm (6 in) square as shown in Figure 6-2. Hammer nails partway into two corners of the wood. With tin snips, cut a strip of

Things you'll need:

- 15 cm x 15 cm (6 in x 6 in) piece of 3/4 in plywood
- hammer
- two nails
- tin snips
- large tin can
- pliers

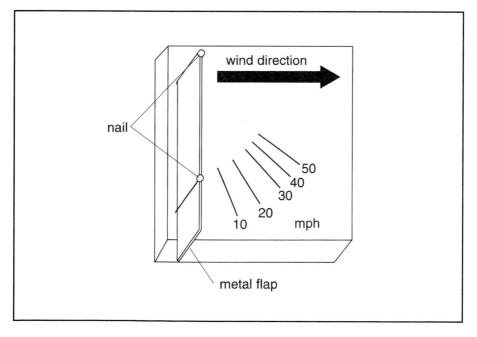

Figure 6-2) Plans for a simple anemometer.

TABLE 1: BEAUFORT SCALE OF WIND SPEED				
	Wind	**(km/h)**	**(mi/h)**	**Visual Observations**
0	Calm	0	0	Smoke rises vertically
1	Light air	1-5	1-3	Wind direction given by smoke but not by wind vane
2	Light breeze	6-11	4-7	Leaves rustle; wind vane moves; can feel wind on your face
3	Gentle breeze	12-19	8-12	Wind extends small flags; leaves in constant motion
4	Moderate breeze	20-29	13-18	Small branches move; dust and loose paper lifted
5	Fresh breeze	30-39	19-24	Small trees with leaves sway; wavelets form on inland waters
6	Strong breeze	40-50	25-31	Large branches moving; utility lines seem to whistle
7	Near Gale	51-61	32-38	Whole trees moving; some difficulty walking into the wind
8	Gale	62-74	39-46	Twigs break off trees; difficult to walk into wind
9	Strong gale	75-87	47-54	Slight damage to buildings
10	Storm	88-102	55-63	Trees uprooted; considerable damage to buildings
11	Violent storm	103-119	64-74	Widespread damage
12	Hurricane	120+	75+	Extreme destruction of property

metal from a tin can. **Be careful not to get cut, the metal can be sharp.** The strip should be about 2.5 cm (1 in) wide and 20 cm (8 in) long. Use pliers to bend one end of the strip around a nail. Draw an arrow on the wood to show which way to aim the anemometer. When the anemometer is pointed into the wind, the strip will be blown up at an angle.

In order to know wind speed, your anemometer must be calibrated.

To do this, you will have to be taken on a short car ride on a calm day. Find a straight road where there is very little traffic. Ask your adult driver to go exactly 16 kmph (10 mph). Hold the anemometer out of the window with the arrow pointing in the direction you are going, and draw a pencil line on the wood to show how high the strip is blown up. Make other lines when the car is traveling 32, 48, 64, and 80 kmph (20, 30, 40, and 50 mph).

Test your anemometer on the next windy day. How much does the wind speed change from one minute to the next?

The Beaufort Scale uses the movement of smoke, leaves, and trees as an estimate of wind speed. You can compare your measurements made with the anemometer with the Beaufort Scale shown in Table 1.

Measuring Rainfall

To measure rainfall you will need a rain gauge. There are several types of rain gauges used at weather stations. One kind has a small tipping bucket mounted on a delicate see-saw. When one side of the bucket becomes filled with rain, it tips down, empties, and moves the other side of the bucket into position for filling. It takes only 0.245 mm (0.01 in) of rain to tip the bucket. Each time the buckets move, an electric signal is sent to a recording drum inside the weather station.

Another kind of rain gauge has a large bucket attached to the top of a weighing scale. As the bucket fills with rainwater, the weight on the scale is recorded by a pen drawing on a piece of paper which is attached to a slowly turning drum.

In your weather station, you can use a simpler rain gauge like the one described in investigation 6.3.

6.3 Make a Rain Gauge*

A rain gauge is merely a container for measuring how much rain falls during a storm. To collect rain you will need a large jar or can with straight sides. (See Figure 6-3). A peanut butter jar or coffee can is perfect, while a mayonnaise jar is not suitable since its mouth is not full-size.

Things you'll need:

- large jar or can with straight sides
- narrow olive jar
- short strip of masking tape
- pencil
- ruler

Because rainfall is reported in increments of 2.45 mm (0.1 inch), light rainfalls would be difficult to measure in your wide-collecting jar or can. For more accurate measurements you need a second jar that

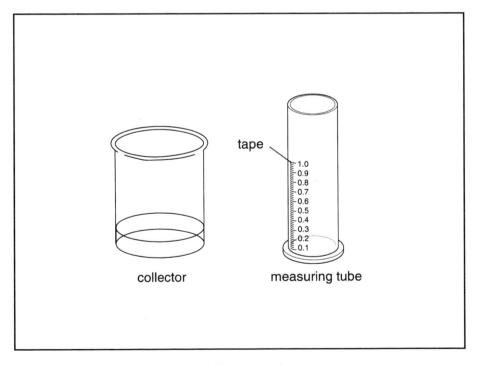

tape

1.0
0.9
0.8
0.7
0.6
0.5
0.4
0.3
0.2
0.1

collector   measuring tube

Figure 6-3) Plans for a rain gauge.

is as narrow as possible. Olives come in jars that are only 5 cm (2 in) in diameter.

To calibrate the narrow measuring jar, pour water into the wide collecting jar until it is exactly 2.5 cm (1 in) deep. Then pour the water from the wide jar into the narrow jar. Use a strip of masking tape to make a scale on the outside of the measuring jar. Mark the height of the water as 2.5 cm (1 in) and divide the space into 10 equal parts for the tenths.

Empty the collecting container and place it outside in an open spot away from trees, bushes, and buildings. You might want to tie the container to a small stake so that it is not upset by the wind or some thirsty animal.

Remember to check your rain gauge every morning, since sometimes it rains at night while you are asleep. When you find rain in the container, untie it and measure the amount of water with the calibrated olive jar. Most storms will deposit less than an inch of rain. If there is more than 2.5 cm (1 in) of rain, empty the first inch from the calibrated jar and continue to measure the water collected.

In winter, when the temperature in the clouds is very cold, snowflakes form and fall instead of rain. It's quite easy to measure a snowfall as you will discover during investigation 6.4. In investigation 6.5 you will learn how to convert the depth of a snowfall into inches of rain.

6.4 Measuring Snow Depth*

All you need to measure the depth of snow is a ruler or yardstick. Go out after the storm and find an open area away from trees and buildings.

Things you'll need:

- ruler or yardstick or meter stick

Push the ruler straight down through the snow until it strikes the hard ground. After reading the depth, shovel away the snow until you have a small bare spot. Now you measure the next snowfall in the same place without the snow layer from the first storm underneath.

6.5 Measuring the Water Content of Snow*

It is important for meteorologists to know the water content of the snow that falls during the winter. When spring arrives in colder climates,

Things you'll need:

- tall coffee can
- ruler

water from melting snow runs into rivers and lakes. If there is a lot of snow or if the snow melts too quickly dangerous floods can result. Fortunately, flood waters often can be controlled by closing dams and later releasing the water more slowly.

To find the water content of snow you need a tall coffee can. Fill the can with loose snow; do not pack it down. Bring the can inside, allow the snow to melt, and measure the depth of water. Then figure out how much snow it would take to equal 2.5 cm (1 in) of water. Compare the melt water made by snow or sleet from different storms.

People often say that 25 cm (10 in) of snow will produce 2.5 cm (1 in) of water. This is rarely true, however. When the snow is dry and fluffy, it might take more than 38 cm (15 in) of snow to make 2.5 cm (1 in) of water. Other times the snow is wet and heavy: perfect for snowball fights and for making snowmen. With slushy snow, 7.4 to 9.8 cm (3 to 4 in) might be enough to melt into 2.5 cm (1 in) of water.

Using Barometers to Measure Air Pressure

As you know, we live at the bottom of an immense 'ocean' of air. Air weighs more than you think; the air in your school classroom probably weighs between 200 and 300 kg (440 and 660 lbs), depending upon the room's size. It is the weight of the air in the atmosphere above you that causes air pressure.

You are not aware of the pressure caused by the air because it is pushing in all directions at the same time. The force caused by the air's weight is only evident if there is a space without air: a vacuum. When you drink with a straw, you create a partial vacuum inside your mouth. Then the air pressure pushes the drink up the straw into your mouth.

The first barometer invented by Torricelli was a tube filled with liquid mercury. The air pressure supported a column of mercury about 76 cm (30 in) high (Figure 1-1b). If he had used water in his barometer, the tube would have had to be over 10.4 m (34 ft) tall. Since mercury is about 14 times heavier than an equal volume of water, the air pressure can support a column of water 14 times as high as a mercury column. Pascal made a barometer filled with wine, but it had to be 14 m (46 ft) long. Which is denser, wine or water?

Barometers without liquid are called aneroid, which means dry. An aneroid barometer has an air-tight metal drum, from which part of the air has been exhausted. A pointer is connected to the side of the drum by sensitive gears and levers. Even small changes in air pressure cause the drum to change shape very slightly. The delicate linkages magnify this motion and transmit it to the pointer on a dial. Although aneroid barometers are not as accurate as mercurial barometers, they can be easily carried from place to place, as you found in Chapter 1.

Most weather stations have recording barometers called barographs. Air pressure readings are continually recorded on a paper-covered cylinder that slowly rotates.

Some science books give plans for making a barometer with a balloon stretched over the neck of a large bottle. Other books show how to make a barometer from a bottle and a short tube filled with water. Unfortunately, such devices are really only thermometers since they respond mostly to variations in temperature rather than air pressure. It is not possible to make a good, homemade barometer.

Perhaps there is already an aneroid barometer in your house. If not, ask if you can buy one at a hardware store or a science museum gift shop. The barometer is one of the most important instruments to have for your weather station.

Airplanes use special barometers, called altimeters, to determine their height when in flight.

Your barometer does not have to be outside to detect changes in air pressure. Even when all your doors and windows are tightly closed, air leaks into and out of your house, keeping the inside pressure exactly the same as the pressure outside.

Just for Fun

- Since water is much heavier than air, water exerts more pressure. You can feel water pressure in a bucket of water. Wrap your arm inside a large plastic bag and reach into the bucket. You will be able to feel the water pressure pushing the bag against your skin. Where is the pressure greatest?

- Try to drink water through a straw that has a hole in the side near the end in your mouth. What happens?

Humidity and Relative Humidity

When water evaporates, it goes into the air, but the particles of water vapor are much too small to see. Humidity is the amount of water vapor in the air. There is a limit to how much vapor the air can hold, and warm air can hold more moisture than cold air. The dew point is the temperature at which the moisture in the air condenses.

Relative humidity is the amount of water vapor the air holds at a certain temperature, compared with the total amount it could hold at that temperature. For example, when the relative humidity is 50%, it means that air contains half of the moisture it could hold at its present temperature. When the relative humidity is 100%, the air contains its maximum amount of water vapor.

Relative humidity usually changes during the day as the air temperature changes from sunrise to sunset, yet the actual amount of vapor in the air remains about the same. In the morning when the air is cooler, the relative humidity might be 75%. Yet when the air warms up by noontime, the relative humidity of the same air could drop to 60%.

Humidity is measured with a hygrometer. During investigation 6.6, you will learn how to make a hygrometer for your weather station.

6.6 Measuring Humidity with a Hygrometer*

Some hygrometers are made with human hair. An increase in humidity causes the hair to increase slightly in length and move a recording device.

It is easier to make a hygrometer with two thermometers, one with a dry bulb and the other with a wet bulb. The dry bulb is just a regular thermometer. The wet bulb thermometer is covered with a piece of moist cloth, which cools the thermometer as the water evaporates. In dry air, the water evaporates rapidly and causes a significant temperature decrease. But in humid air, evaporation occurs more slowly, and there is a smaller decline in temperature.

To make your hygrometer, cut a piece of shoe lace about 6 in (15 cm) long, and slip the cut end over the bulb of one thermometer. Hold the thermometers to the milk carton with rubber bands as shown

Things you'll need:

- two alcohol thermometers
- shoe lace
- empty milk carton
- rubber bands
- water
- small piece of cardboard

in Figure 6-4. Cut a hole in the carton near the lace, and push the lace through the hole so that it rests on the bottom. Then pour water into the carton to keep the lace wet.

Before using the hygrometer, be sure the lace around the thermometer bulb is wet. To make a reading on your hygrometer, use a small piece of stiff cardboard to fan the wet bulb continually for five minutes. Then quickly read the temperatures on both thermometers, and write them down in your notebook. Subtract the wet bulb temperature reading from the dry bulb reading to find the difference in the temperatures.

Now you can figure out the relative humidity by using Table 2. Find the temperature closest to the dry bulb temperature at the left side of the table. Next, find the number at the top of the table that matches the difference you found between the wet bulb and the dry bulb

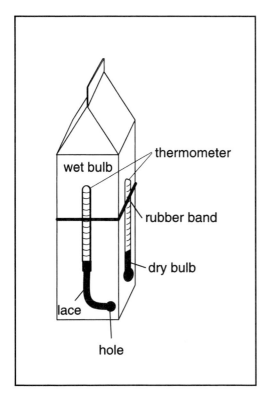

Figure 6-4) Plans for a hygrometer.

TABLE 2: FINDING THE RELATIVE HUMIDITY (PERCENT)

Using Fahrenheit Temperatures—Dry Difference in Temperature (dry bulb—wet bulb temp)

Bulb	1	2	3	4	5	6	7	8	9	10	11	12	13	14	15	16	17	18	19	20	25	30
0	67	33																				
5	73	46	20																			
10	78	56	34	13																		
15	82	64	46	29	11																	
20	85	70	55	40	26	12																
25	87	74	62	49	37	25	13															
30	89	78	67	56	46	36	26	16														
35	91	81	72	63	54	45	36	27	19	10												
40	92	83	75	68	60	52	45	37	29	22	15											
45	93	86	78	71	64	57	51	44	38	31	25	18	12									
50	93	87	80	74	67	61	55	49	43	38	32	27	21	16	10							
55	94	88	82	76	70	65	59	54	49	43	38	33	28	23	19	14						
60	94	89	83	78	73	68	63	58	53	48	43	39	34	30	26	21	17	13				
65	95	90	85	80	75	70	66	61	56	52	48	44	39	35	31	27	24	20	16	12		
70	95	90	86	81	77	72	68	64	59	55	51	48	44	40	36	33	29	25	22	19		
75	96	91	86	82	78	74	70	66	62	58	54	51	47	44	40	37	34	30	27	24		
80	96	91	87	83	79	75	72	68	64	61	57	54	50	47	44	41	38	35	32	29	15	
85	96	92	88	84	80	76	73	69	66	62	59	56	52	49	46	43	41	38	35	32	20	
90	96	92	89	85	81	78	74	71	68	65	61	58	55	52	49	47	44	41	39	36	24	
95	96	93	89	85	82	79	75	72	69	66	63	60	57	54	51	49	46	43	41	38	27	
100	96	93	89	86	83	80	77	73	70	68	65	62	59	56	54	51	49	46	44	41	30	21

USING CELSIUS TEMPERATURES																
Dry Difference in Temperature (dry bulb temp—wet bulb temp)																
Bulb	0.5	1.0	1.5	2.0	2.5	3.0	3.5	4.0	4.5	5.0	7.5	10.0	12.5	15	17.5	20
-15	79	79	58	38	18											
-12.5	82	65	47	30	13											
-10	85	69	54	39	24	10										
-7.5	87	73	60	48	35	22	10									
-5	88	77	66	54	43	32	21	11								
-2.5	90	80	70	60	50	42	37	22	12							
0	91	82	73	65	56	47	39	31	23	15						
2.5	92	84	76	68	61	53	46	38	31	24						
5	93	86	78	71	65	58	51	45	38	32						
7.5	93	87	80	74	68	62	56	50	44	38						
10	94	88	82	76	71	65	60	54	49	44	19					
12.5	94	89	84	78	73	68	63	58	53	48	25					
15	95	90	85	80	75	70	66	61	57	52	31	12				
17.5	95	90	86	81	77	72	68	64	60	55	36	18				
20	95	91	87	82	78	74	70	66	62	58	40	24				
22.5	96	92	87	83	80	76	72	68	64	61	44	28	14			
25	96	92	88	84	81	77	73	70	66	63	47	32	19			
27.5	96	92	89	85	82	78	75	71	68	65	50	36	23	12		
30	96	93	89	86	82	79	76	73	70	67	52	39	27	16		
32.5	97	93	90	86	83	80	77	74	71	68	54	42	30	20	11	
35	97	93	90	87	84	81	78	75	72	69	56	44	33	23	14	
37.5	97	94	91	87	85	82	79	76	73	70	58	46	36	26	18	10
40	97	94	91	88	85	82	79	77	74	72	59	48	38	29	21	13

temperatures. The percent of relative humidity is given where the dry temperature row intersects the temperature difference column. For example, if the dry bulb temperature is 60°F and the wet bulb temperature is 50°F, then the humidity is 48 percent.

Your Weather Watch

Try to assemble as many weather instruments as you can. You do not need to have all of the instruments described above in order to become a good weather watcher.

You should make a paper chart for recording your daily measurements and observations. Make separate columns for date and time, temperature, wind direction and speed, rain or snow fall amounts, air pressure, relative humidity, and clouds. You might want to compare your measurements with the reports of weather conditions given in newspapers and on television news programs.

Forecasting the weather is not easy, but the next chapter provides some tips that will help you. These tips together with the information gathered at your weather station will improve your weather forecasting skills.

7

Making Weather Forecasts

Now that you have your own weather station, you can make local weather forecasts based on the information obtained from your instruments and other sources. We will provide some suggestions to help you get started. With experience your forecasts will probably become more accurate. (Do not worry about making mistakes, even the forecasts of professional meteorologists are correct only about 70 percent of the time.)

As you begin making forecasts, you will find that the most useful data come from barometer readings, wind directions, and cloud types.

Clouds as Weather Indicators

- Cirrus clouds, if ahead of a warm front, indicate rain within 24–48 hours. Cirrus clouds followed by increasingly lower clouds helps to confirm the prediction.

- Cumulus clouds that develop in the afternoon indicate fair weather unless they become increasingly dense like thunderheads, which may indicate an electrical storm within a few hours.

- Patchy, high cirrus clouds in the west generally indicate fair weather. However, if these clouds lower, thicken, and move from the south or southwest while an east wind is blowing at ground level, rain may follow within a day. The fusion of high clouds moving from the south or southwest with an east wind at ground level indicates rain and a southwest wind within a few hours.

- Dark lowering clouds moving from the south or southwest with southeast ground winds suggest steady rain is approaching.

- Dark thunderheads with bases that are nearly jet black and building upward indicates severe weather, with possible hail and tornadoes.

- Rounded white clouds, if surrounded by open sky and moving in the same direction as the ground wind, indicates fair weather. Should these clouds fuse to cover the sky or grow into thunderheads, rain is likely.

In general, you can anticipate bad weather if:

- high clouds increase, thicken and lower;

- fast-moving clouds do the same;

- clouds develop dark bases;

- the sky is filled with clouds moving in different directions at the same time;

- middle level clouds darken in the west;

- heavy clouds build upward on a warm summer morning;

- low-level, fast-moving clouds are coming from the east or south.

On the other hand, good weather can be expected when:

- there is a decrease in the cloud cover;

- breaks appear in the clouds, particularly in the morning hours;

- when there is a ground fog that disappears during the morning.

Other Weather Indicators
Useful in Making Forecasts

Fair weather can be expected to continue when:

- the pressure indicated by your barometer is steady or rising;

- your thermometer shows that the temperature is steady and normal for the season;

- your weather vane shows steady, gentle winds from the west or northwest;

- the sun sets in a clear or reddish sky;

- dew or frost is present in the morning.

A *storm* is likely when:

- your barometer indicates a steady decline of the air pressure and your weather vane shows the wind is coming from the south, southeast, or east;

- a falling barometric pressure is accompanied by a wind from the east or northeast, suggesting a storm from the south or southeast;

- the wind shifts to the south or east;

- a north wind shifts counterclockwise (from north to west to south);

- you find that the temperature and humidity are both rising and that the wind is from the south or east;

- the sun sets behind cirrus clouds;

- there is a ring (halo) around the moon.

Clearing weather can be anticipated when:

- your weather vane shows the wind shifting to the west;

- your barometer indicates that the air pressure is rising rapidly;

- the cloud ceiling rises.

Cooler weather can be expected when:

- air pressure rises;

- the wind shifts to the north or northwest;

- winter clouds break and there is a greenish tint in the northern sky;

- a cold front is known to be approaching from the northwest or west;

- the sky is clear at night and the wind is calm.

Warmer weather can be anticipated if:

- clouds cover the night sky;

- the wind shifts to the south or southwest;

- a warm front is approaching.

Weather Maps

Meteorologists have access to weather maps prepared from information gathered from hundreds of weather stations. The surface data from each station is summarized by a set of symbols shown in Figure 7-1. On the basis of the data collected from hundreds of weather stations across the country, a national weather map can be updated periodically.

Using the data from all the weather stations, a national weather map is prepared. Isobars (equal pressure lines) and isotherms (equal temperature lines) are drawn using the data supplied by the many local weather stations.

Weather maps also show the positions of weather fronts—places where large air masses collide. For example, a cold air mass from northern Canada may collide with a warmer air mass to the south. The cold air will push under the warmer air and lift it. If the cold air

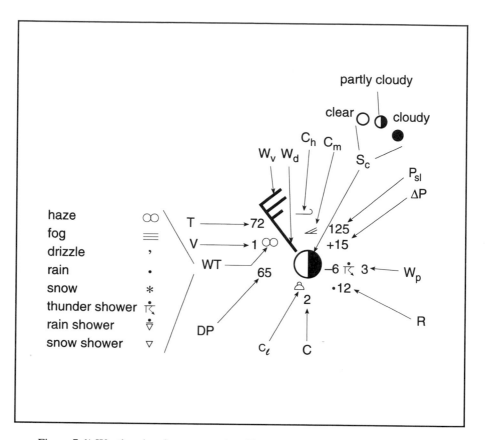

Figure 7-1) Weather data from one station. The symbols, reading clockwise from 11 o'clock are W_v = wind velocity in knots (1 knot = 1.15 mph); W_d = wind direction (W_v symbols are tail of arrow); C_h = type of high clouds; C_m = type of middle height clouds. S_c = sky cover; P_{sl} = air pressure in millibars at sea level; ΔP = change in air pressure in past 3 hours (+ indicates rise, / indicates steady rise); W_p = weather over past 6 hours (-6) and the time it ended or started (3 hours ago); R = precipitation in last 6 hours; C = ceiling (height of lowest clouds); C_l = low cloud type; D_p = dew point in °F; W_T = type of weather (see various symbols); V = visibility; T = temperature in °F.

advances, we have a cold front. If the air masses do not move, we have a stationary front. If the cold air retreats as warm air moves over it, we have a warm front. Finally, an occluded front occurs when a cold front, which generally moves faster than a warm front, overtakes a warm front and lifts the warmer air. The symbols used to indicate these fronts are shown in Figure 7-2.

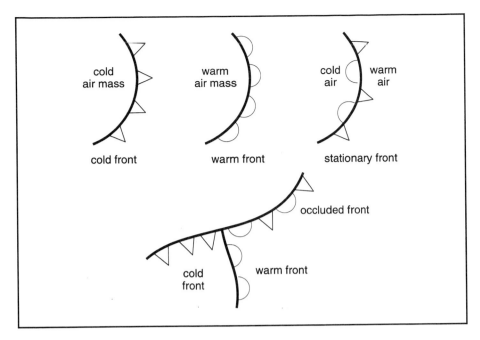

Figure 7-2) Weather fronts.

Weather Fronts

The passage of weather fronts is usually accompanied by bad or unsettled weather. Fronts are generally found along a low-pressure trough; consequently the pressure drops as the front approaches and then rises after it has passed. In the Northern Hemisphere, ground winds shift clockwise as the front passes. By watching the movement of weather fronts from day to day, you can often predict when cooler or warmer weather will arrive. Generally, cold fronts move at an average speed of 32 kmp (20 mph) and warm fronts move about 24 kmp (15 mph).

When a warm front advances into a cold air mass, the warm air rises over the cold air as shown in Figure 7-3a. As a result, the upper air weather induced by the warm air extends hundreds of kilometers (miles) ahead of the front at ground level. High cirrus clouds often indicate an approaching warm front. If there is a moon in the night sky, moonlight passing through the ice crystals that make up these high

117

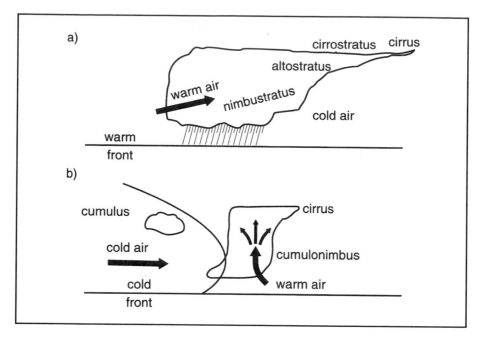

Figure 7-3a) Warm front. 7-3b) Cold front.

clouds may give rise to a halo, in much the same way that sunlight passing through rain produces rainbows. Behind the cirrus clouds, clouds thicken gradually and descend. If conditions are right, rain may fall several hundred kilometers (miles) behind the advancing cirrus clouds.

In the United States, cold fronts generally arrive from the northwest and move eastward or southeastward. The colder, denser air in a cold front wedges under the warm air into which it moves, pushing the warm air above it. Friction between air and ground holds back the cold surface air while higher air advances faster. This gives rise to the steep, rounded shape of the cold front shown in Figure 7-3b. The steep slope causes warm air to rise rapidly. As a result, the storms that accompany a fast-moving cold front are often brief but violent. The storms that accompany a slow-moving cold front tend to be longer and less violent.

Air Pressure and Weather

High-pressure cells develop anywhere that air cools, compresses, and sinks. In the Northern Hemisphere, this happens most commonly around the horse latitudes (30°N) and near the North Pole. As the air settles, it moves clockwise and outward toward lower pressure, and is twisted to the right by the Coriolis effect. These high pressure regions are usually several hundred kilometers (miles) in diameter, but they may stretch out over several thousand kilometers (miles).

Large regions of low pressure develop in a complicated fashion between two high-pressure air masses that are at different temperatures. Local low-pressure cells, about 32 km (20 mi) in diameter, develop when warm air rises. Air at higher pressure moves toward the warm, low-pressure air, twisting counterclockwise as it goes because of the Coriolis effect and friction with the ground. Larger lows, such as those found over the deserts of western Arizona and southeastern California, may form by the same process.

The velocity of the clockwise winds around a high pressure cell and the counterclockwise winds around a low pressure cell depends on the intensity of the pressure differences. Where the isobars are close together, the wind velocity will be high. The closeness of the isobars indicates that the pressure changes sharply. The winds will be lighter where the isobars are farther apart. In general, high pressure is associated with fair weather and low pressure with cloudy or damp weather. Air that is saturated with water vapor is less dense than dry air, because water molecules have less mass than the nitrogen and oxygen molecules that make up dry air.

Exploring on Your Own

- On a national weather map keep a daily record of the postion of storm centers as they move across the country. Do these storm centers move faster in the summer or in the winter? Or does the season have no effect on the rate at which they move?

APPENDIX
Suppliers of Materials

The following companies supply materials needed for the experiments in this book.

Carolina Biological Supply Co.
2700 York Road
Burlington, NC 27215
(800) 334-5551;
http://www.carolina.com

Central Scientific Co. (CENCO)
3300 Cenco Parkway
Franklin Park, IL 60131
(800) 262-3626;
http://www.cenconet.com

Connecticut Valley Biological
Supply Co., Inc.
82 Valley Road, Box 326
Southampton, MA 01073
(800) 628-7748

Delta Education
P.O. Box 915
Hudson, NH 03051-0915
(800) 258-1302

Edmund Scientific Co.
101 East Gloucester Pike
Barrington, NJ 08007
(609) 547-3488

Educational Innovations, Inc.
151 River Road
Cos Cob, CT 06807-2514
http://www.teachersource.com

Fisher Science Education
485 S. Frontage Road
Burr Ridge, IL 60521
(800) 955-4663
http://www.fisheredu.com

Frey Scientific
100 Paragon Parkway
Mansfield, OH 44903
(800) 225-3739

Nasco-Fort Atkinson
P.O. Box 901
Fort Atkinson, WI 53538-0901
(800) 558-9595

Nasco-Modesto
P.O. Box 3837
Modesto, CA 95352-3837
(800) 558-9595
http://www.nascofa.com

Sargent-Welch/VWR Scientific
P.O. Box 5229
Buffalo Grove, IL 60089-5229
(800) SAR-GENT
http://www.SargentWelch.com

Science Kit & Boreal Laboratories
777 East Park Drive
Tonawanda, NY 14150
(800) 828-7777
http://sciencekit.com

Ward's Natural Science
Establishment, Inc.
P.O. Box 92912
Rochester, NY 14692-9012
(800) 962-2660
http://www.wardsci.com

Bibliography

"An Introduction to Weather." Washington, D.C.: *National Geographic,* 1981.

Asimov, Isaac. *How Did We Find Out About the Atmosphere.* New York: Walker, 1985.

Beller, Joel. *So You Want to Do a Science Project.* New York: Arco, 1982.

Bombaugh, Ruth. *Science Fair Success, Revised and Expanded.* Springfield, N.J.: Enslow Publishers, Inc., 1999.

DeBruin, Jerry. *Young Scientists Explore the Weather.* Carthage, Ill.: Good Apple, 1983.

Gardner, R., and D. Webster. *Science in Your Backyard.* New York: Messner, 1987.

Ludlum, David M. *The American Weather Book.* Boston: Houghton-Mifflin, 1982.

Mitchell-Christie, Frank. *Practical Weather Forecasting.* Woodbury, N.Y.: Barron's, 1978.

Tocci, Salvatore. *How to Do a Science Fair Project.* New York: Watts, 1986.

Van Deman, B.A., and E. MacDonald. *Nuts and Bolts: A Matter of Fact Guide to Science Fair Projects.* Harwood Heights, Ill.: Science Man Press, 1980.

Webster, David. *How to Do a Science Project.* New York: Watts, 1974.

Internet Addresses

The World Wide Web offers access to various types of information on science projects and experiments about weather. In some cases you can view actual experiments or even replicate them yourself. Information is generally very current, often available without a trip to a library, and relatively easy to find.

Just as it is important to put safety first when conducting science experiments, it is also essential that you search the Web in a safe fashion and that you be critical of information you retrieve using a search engine. With over one billion indexable web sites to choose from, it is difficult to find exactly what you need and to determine that the information is reputable and authoritative. While a search engine may retrieve some useful sites, it may also overwhelm you with thousands of possibilities, many of which may be inaccurate, out-of-date, or inappropriate to your topic.

This chapter identifies and describes some of the best, most reputable, and stable sites on the web which can help you when considering doing a science project on some aspect of weather.

Internet Addresses researched by: Greg Byerly and Carolyn S. Brodie are Associate Professors in the School of Library and Information Science, Kent State University and write a monthly Internet column titled COMPUTER CACHE for *School Library Media Activities Monthly.*

Web Sites with Information on Weather

Franklin's Forecast
http://sln.fi.edu/weather/index.html
This site from Franklin Institute Online shows you how to build your own weather station and explains various weather events. Learn about radar's role in weather forecasts, view some pictures of lightning, and try some of the suggested weather activities.

Hurricanes
http://www.fema.gov/kids/hurr.htm
This site from the Federal Emergency Management Agency (FEMA) explains how hurricanes are named and classified.

How the Weather Service Gets the Word Out
http://www.nws.noaa.gov/wordout.shtml
Provides information on how weather forecasting and prediction information is disseminated to the public from the National Weather Service. Learn about and link to different weather information services available, including NOAA weather radio, climate data, and weather by telephone.

Making a Weather Station
http://www.miamisci.org/hurricane/weatherstation.html
Learn how to build your own weather tools including a barometer, thermometer, anemometer, and rain gauge. Then use these tools by keeping track of weather measurements related to wind, moisture, air pressure and temperature.

National Climactic Data Center
http://www.ncdc.noaa.gov/ncdc.html
The NCDC, a part of the National Oceanic and Atmospheric Administration (NOAA), provides access to the world's largest active archive of weather data from around the world. Use these weather maps and graphical information to analyze and compare international weather data.

National Oceanic and Atmospheric Administration (NOAA)
http://www.noaa.gov/
As the federal agency responsible for oceanic and atmospheric research, NOAA sponsors and produces many weather-related web sites.

National Snow and Ice Data Center
http://nsidc.org/NSIDC/EDUCATION/
Bundle up and learn about snow and ice research. Topics covered include snow cover, avalanches, glaciers, ice sheets, freshwater ice, sea ice, ground ice, permafrost, atmospheric ice, paleoglaciology, and ice cores.

National Weather Service
http://www.nws.noaa.gov/
As the official weather warning service of the United States, the National Weather Service provides "warnings and forecast of hazardous weather, including thunderstorms, flooding, hurricanes, tornadoes, winter weather, tsunamis, and climate events." Use the general information section for weather-related topics, compiled weather data, and links to commercial meteorological web sites.

Penn State University Weather Pages
http://www.ems.psu.edu/wx/

View high-resolution hourly satellite images and surface analyses of temperature, dewpoint, wind, and moisture for northeast United States.

Tornado Project Online
http://www.tornadoproject.com/

The site offers stories about tornado oddities, personal experiences from tornado survivors, and descriptions of historic tornadoes as well as more recent tornadoes. The site also features summary tables of the Fujita (F) scale for estimating tornado damage, top ten lists of the most damaging tornadoes, and instructions for making a tornado simulator.

USA Today Weather
http://www.usatoday.com/weather/wfront.htm

The Online Weather Almanac gives facts and figures about weather and climate across the United States and around the world. Weather basics are described with good graphics and various weather phenomena, like thunderstorms, tornadoes or hurricanes, are explained in some detail.

The Weather Calculator
http://www.srh.noaa.gov/elp/wxcalc/wxcalc.html

Want to calculate the heat index or the wind chill? What about relative humidity or vapor pressure? These and many other weather calculations are available at this site. You can even convert cricket chirps into the current Fahrenheit temperature.

Weather Underground
http://www.wunderground.com/

One of the original weather sites on the web, the Weather Underground continues to be a good source of current weather information. Consult current national maps for temperature, visibility, wind, heat index, windchill, humidity, and dewpoint. General weather conditions are provided for major cities around the world.

Weather: What Forces Affect our Weather?
http://www.learner.org/exhibits/weather/

A part of the Annenberg/CPB learner.org site, this site investigates what physical phenomena affect our weather. Consider the impact of the atmosphere, water, storms, and ice and snow have on weather. You can interactively try tornado chasing or investigate how wind chill works. Each section includes links to other weather topics.

Weather World
http://members.aol.com/Accustiver/wxworld.html
This is a comprehensive weather site with worldwide forecasts, weather images and graphics, and weather watches and warnings. The Weather Extras section includes a list of weather calculation sites, downloadable weather software, and links to over 800 weather cams. There is also a large collection of weather folklore.

WW2010 Weather Project
http://ww2010.atmos.uiuc.edu/(Gh)/home.rxml
This site combines good information about all aspects of weather with some of the best satellite images and weather data. WW2010 automatically generates over 3,500 forecast weather maps every 24 hours using standard radar, satellite images, and computer forecast models.

Science Fairs

Science Fair Central
http://school.discovery.com/sciencefaircentral/
Part of the Discovery Channel School site, Science Fair Central is a great place to begin researching a science project. The Science Fair Studio includes a detailed handbook on the steps in a science project which is based on the print publication, *A Guide to the Best Science Fair Projects*, by Janice VanCleave. Check out Jake's Attic which features a different experiment each month.

Science Fair Projects Index
http://www.ascpl.lib.oh.us/scifair/sftp.htm
This site is an electronic database prepared by the Akron-Summit County (OH) Public Library of science fair projects which have been included in books dating from 1990 to the present. Since the books must be consulted to get further information about the projects, this site is best used when trying to pick a topic or to see if your idea has already been done. The projects may be searched by subject, experiment title or grade level.

SciFair.org
http://www.scifair.org/
Also known as the Ultimate Science Fair Resource, this site includes articles on project steps, project hints, the scientific method, writing reports, and display boards. You can use the Idea Bank to brainstorm about possible topics and then share your ideas with others on the Idea Board.

Your Science Fair Project Resource Guide
http://www.ipl.org/youth/projectguide/
This instructional guide from the Internet Public Library covers: choosing a topic, sample projects, resources, and ask an expert. Basic information is provided and accompanied by links to other science-related sites.

General Science Web Sites

Bill Nye the Science Guy's Nye Labs Online
http://nyelabs.kcts.org/
This is the online lab for this popular TV show. Bill Nye, the Science Guy, makes science fun, but he also suggests real experiments and projects you can try at home.

Exploratorium
http://www.exploratorium.edu/
The Exploratorium is an online "museum of science, art, and human perception." Search the archives to find collections of past exhibitions, digital images, archived webcasts, and webcam sites. The Exploratorium is best known for its cow's eye dissection, but it includes many other interactive science activities.

Math & Science Gateway
http://www.tc.cornell.edu/Edu/MathSciGateway/
This comprehensive site provides "links to resources in mathematics and science for educators and students in grades 9–12." Subjects covered include biology, chemistry, the environment, health, mathematics, and physics.

The Science Page
http://www.sciencepage.org/
Another good collection of science and science education sites which can be used to research a wide range of science topics, including weather, chemistry, physics, and biology. Check out the science fair projects and the activities, labs, and lesson plans. A unique aspect of the site is its collection of science analogies.

Index

A absorption of radiation
by water and soil, 47–48
acid rain, 40
air
and density, 59–60
and pressure, 59–60
and wind, 56–77
volume and temperature, 66–68
weighing, 57–59
air pressure, 12, 64
and altitude, 14–17
and barometer, 105–106
and wind, 65
anemometer, 99–101
aneroid barometer, 12–13
atmosphere, 9–25
and pressure, 14–17
and temperature, 14
as a sea of air, 11
composition of, 20–25
earth's, 19–21
on other planets, 17–19

B barometer
and air pressure, 105–106
aneroid, 12–13
bibliography, 126
Buys Ballot's Rule, 77

C condensation, 30
convection, 48–50
Coriolis effect, 76–77
clouds
formation of, 31–32
kinds of, 33–35
seeding, 36
watching, 35–36

D dust devils, 90–91

E earth
evolution of, 26
evaporation, 28–29

F forecasts, 112–119
and clouds, 112–113
helpful indicators, 114–115

H hail, 40–41
humidity, 106–111
hurricanes, 91–94
and safety, 94
damage by, 93–94
formation of, 91–93
warnings of, 94
hygrometer, 107–111

J jet stream, 75

L latitude, 54–55
lightning, 80–81

M meteorologists, 10

O oxygen, 21–25
as a fraction of air, 21–25
ozone, 21

P Pascal, Blaise, 14, 62
pressure, 59–62
prism, 39

R radiation, 46–48
rainbows, 38–39
raindrops, 36–38
rainfall
measuring, 101
rain gauge, 101–102
relative humidity, 106–111

S safety, 6–7

science fairs, 6
seasons, 50–55
   and earth's axis, 52–53
   cause of, 53–54
snow, 41–42
   measuring depth, 104
   water content, 104
spectroscope, 19
storms, 78–94
Sun, 43–55
   temperature of, 43

T temperature
   and time of day, 46
   inversion, 14
   on earth, 44–46
   on moon, 44–45
   on sun and planets, 43–45
thermometer, 95–96
thunderstorms, 78–83
   and damage, 82–83
   and safety, 83
   development of, 78–79
   distance to, 82
   distribution, 79–80
   thunder and lightning, 80–81
tornadoes, 83–90
   and safety, 89–90
   damage from, 88–89
   formation of, 86–87
troposphere, 14

W water
   hot and cold, 63
   temperature and density,
      63–64
water cycle, 26–28
waterspouts, 90
weather
   and air pressure, 118–119
   and meteorologists, 10
   forecasts, 112–119
      and clouds, 112–113
      helpful indicators, 114–115
   fronts, 117–118

   instruments, 96–111
      anemometer, 99–101
      barometer, 105–106
      hygrometer, 106–111
      thermometer, 95–96
      wind vane, 97–98
   maps, 115–116
   station, 95–111
   stormy, 78–94
weather station, 95–111
   instruments, 96–111
weighing air, 57–59
wind
   across earth, 70–74
   and air, 56–77
   and jet stream, 75
   direction, 96–98
   local, 68–69
   speed, 96–101

V vane, 97–98